Drawn By His Love
The Life of Holiness

Drawn By His Love

The Life of Holiness

by Jerry Savelle

HARRISON HOUSE
Tulsa, Oklahoma

Cover Photo by Picture Works
Broken Arrow, Oklahoma

Drawn by His Love — The Life of Holiness
ISBN 0-89274-459-6
Copyright © 1987 by Jerry Savelle
P. O. Box 2228
Fort Worth, Texas 76113

Published by Harrison House, Inc.
P. O. Box 35035
Tulsa, Oklahoma 74153

Contents

1
A Fresh Beginning

Today the Spirit of God is on the move in a mighty way. You may have sensed in your spirit that God is saying something to you about your own life. Perhaps He has been saying that it is time to start cleaning it up. He may be dealing with you about separating yourself from certain things. You may have begun to notice that your desires are changing.

If so, you are not alone. What you are experiencing is a move of God in the hearts and lives of His people throughout the length and breadth of this land. That movement has to do with a return to something which was begun in the days of the Early Church, something which we have neglected in recent years but which is vitally important to the Church of Jesus Christ in these last climactic days.

Acts Unfinished

For some time now, the Spirit of God has been dealing with me very strongly about something. It began back in September, 1982, while I was ministering in Kenya, East Africa.

A few years ago I was privileged to be the founder of a work in that nation — a church which can now handle 2,000 people. Our headquarters church there in the jungles of Kenya is the talk of the whole area. Because of its dynamic witness, there is excitement in the air all around it.

The mayor, the district commissioner, the chief of police are all excited about the church and its influence upon the community. They can hardly believe all that has happened as a result of its being established there. These officials and others come to our meetings there and testify to the positive influence of the church and its work.

"Before the Gospel was preached in this city," said a former mayor, who had become a Christian himself, "we didn't even have a paved road." Then he went on to cite all the changes brought about since the mission work was begun. He attributed all success and all prosperity in that remote area to the preaching of the Gospel.

Truly God is doing some great things all over that part of Africa. Our ministry alone has a total of 54 national pastors on staff, serving 42 churches which have been established as an outgrowth of our mission in the area.

While I was there visiting these pastors and seeing the progress being made, I was involved in several meetings. Over there, you don't just preach one or two times a day, as we do here in the States. Those people are so hungry for the Word of God, they will stay as long as anyone will preach to them — all day or all night, if necessary.

I had preached in several meetings one day, and came back to my hotel room in the late afternoon exhausted. I decided to lie down for a few minutes to rest for a while before the evening services began. As soon as my head hit the pillow, I dropped off into a deep sleep. I was sleeping soundly when all of a sudden I distinctly heard the Spirit of God say to me, "Get up."

So I got up.

"Read the book of Acts."

"But, Lord," I protested, "I'm tired. I've only been asleep a few minutes. Besides, I've already read the book of Acts."

"I know," the Lord answered. Then He repeated His command, "Read the book of Acts!"

"I don't understand this," I thought to myself as I began to flip through my Bible, "I've read Acts several times; it's a wonderful book. I really enjoyed it. But why do I have to wake up from a sound sleep and read it right now? Have they added a new chapter to it or something since I last read it?"

"Read it again," said the Lord, as though answering my silent questions. "Set a diary by your side, and write down every impulse and every impression you receive in your spirit as you read verse upon verse, line upon line, precept upon precept."

So in obedience to the Lord, I began rereading the book of Acts, making notes as I went along. As I read, to my surprise I began to see things in it I had never noticed before. It was almost as though it had become a new book to me. There were things in there that God brought to my attention I just could not believe I had missed all those times I thought I had read it. But the thing the Lord impressed upon me most was simply this: *God is not through with the book of Acts.* The final chapters of Acts have not been written yet. We Christians are writing them today!

Total Consecration

As members of the same Body of Christ as the first-century disciples, there

are some things in the book of Acts that
we have stopped doing that we need to
begin anew. Now I don't mean to imply
that we should go back and do everything
the Early Church did. Because if we did
that, we would become a baby Church
again, an infant Church.

We must remember that on the day of
Pentecost the Church was just being
born, it was just beginning. We have
made a lot of spiritual progress since
then. We have learned some important
truths in the nearly twenty centuries that
have passed since those early beginnings
of the Church. We know and practice
some things those early believers didn't;
things we need to hold onto.

But there are also some things that
were of vital importance to the Early
Church that the modern-day Church has
neglected. There are some principles,
some traits, some spiritual applications
that were a part of the Early Church
which we need to reinstate today. These
are what the Lord began to show me as
I reread the book of Acts.

"Son," He told me, "I am about to move upon My people in a new way. I am going to demand of them total consecration."

"There are a few things that have taken place over the past few years that I have had to close My eyes to and not look upon," He said. "There have been some things that I have had to turn My head away from and not take notice of. My people have been experiencing a grace period, much like an insurance policy. I have allowed some things to go unchecked. I've overlooked some things. But I'm not going to overlook them anymore.

"Now I am demanding that My people come into the place to which I have called them, regardless of how hard it may be upon their flesh. If they don't do as I command, the policy will lapse."

Dealing with Sin

Then the Lord began to share some things with me. The first thing He revealed to me concerned my own life. He began to bring to light some things in my life that were not pleasing to Him, things I had sort of swept under the rug. I knew they were there all along. From time to time they would pop up, I'd yield to them, and then feel sorry I had done so. So I'd go before the Lord and ask forgiveness. And He would forgive me.

But then when that opportunity to sin would arise again, once more I would yield to temptation. Then I would confess my sin and ask forgiveness. And God would forgive me of it.

Then after a while the temptation to sin came again, and again I yielded to it. I asked God to forgive me. But this time He said to me, "Son, I forgive you, but I didn't give you 1 John 1:9 and 1 John 2:1 so you could keep on sinning."

I was shocked. I recalled these verses to my mind: **If we confess our sins, he is faithful and just to forgive us our sins, and to cleanse us from all unrighteousness** (1 John 1:9). **My little**

children, these things write I unto you, that ye sin not. And if any man sin, we have an advocate with the Father, Jesus Christ the righteous (1 John 2:1).

As I reflected on these scriptures and God's word to me, I began to understand what He was telling me. God was saying that He did not give His children these provisions for us to use as a license to continue in sin. I remembered the words of the Apostle Paul in Romans 6:1,2:

> **What shall we say then? Shall we continue in sin, that grace may abound?**
>
> **God forbid. How shall we, that are dead to sin, live any longer therein?**

God expects us to do something about sin.

We have gone from one extreme to the other. There was a period of time when all we heard preached was sin, sin, sin. We talked about it so much that finally everybody knew how to do it well! We were so convinced that God had said we were all sinners that we didn't want to make Him out a liar by our actions!

But then we got hold of the message of justification. We learned that we have been made the righteousness of God. Praise the Lord for that revelation. Thank God that we have been made righteous. But just because we have been made righteous does not mean that we have become immune to sin.

To be righteous simply means to be in right standing with God. We have that right standing with Him. Because of our relationship with the righteous Father, He expects us as His children to do something about sin. Keeping sin out of our life is something we have to do daily.

At one point we majored on sin; we all saw ourselves as "sinners saved by grace." We held on to that old tag until we identified ourselves more as sinners than we did as saints. Fortunately, most of us have learned not to do that anymore. We learned the truth, that in Christ we have been made the righteousness of God. (2 Cor. 5:21.)

(If you still think of yourself as "just an old sinner saved by grace," then you need a new concept of yourself. If you were indeed saved by grace, then you are not a sinner anymore, you are a child of God. And God doesn't have any "sinners" in His family! If you have been washed in the blood of Jesus Christ, then you are not "an old sinner." You have been given a new identity. According to 2 Corinthians 5:21, through the substitutionary death of Christ, you have been **made the righteousness of God in him.** You need to learn to identify more with your Savior than with your sin.)

Now that does not mean that we Christians cannot sin. Even as the children of God, the righteousness of God, we still have the ability and the opportunity to sin.

Although we have been made the righteousness of God in Christ, we should not put ourselves above our Lord. Even Jesus had the ability and opportunity to sin. The Bible says that He was **in all points tempted like as we are, yet without sin** (Heb. 4:15).

If Jesus had not had the ability and opportunity to sin, He would never have been tempted by Satan. Nor would He have won the victory over His temptation. According to James 1:13, **God cannot be tempted with evil.** That's one reason Jesus had to become a man like us, so He could be tempted in all points like as we are.

Yet Jesus did something we have not always done. He overcame the tempter. Every time. He had many opportunities to sin, but He passed them by. Why? Because He knew that sin is displeasing to God. That is the message that God was giving to me, for myself and for the Body of Christ. He was telling me just what He spoke to us so long ago through the Apostle Paul:

> **Neither yield ye your members as instruments of unrighteousness unto sin: but yield yourselves unto God, as those that are alive from the dead, and your members as instruments of righteousness unto God.**
>
> **Romans 6:13**

Knowing that we are human, that we are not yet perfect, God has made provision for our weakness and our failure. When we do sin, we have an advocate, the Lord Jesus Christ, Who **ever liveth to make intercession for** (us) (Heb. 7:25).

Because of what Christ has done for us, we can go before God, confess our sin, and receive forgiveness of that sin.

God has promised that if we will confess our sin, He is faithful and just to forgive us our sin and cleanse us of all unrighteousness. Thank God we are forever free of our old "sin consciousness."

But the problem is, we have gone from one extreme to the other.

Before, we were majoring on sin and everybody had a sin consciousness; we could hardly realize that we were the righteousness of God because we heard sin preached at us so much. Then we got so "liberated" from sin, we don't even talk about it at all anymore, especially in the "faith circles."

If you mention sin in the faith circles, some people don't think you are a "faith person."

"Did he say 'sin'? Why, bless God, we live by faith."

That's true. But living by faith does not mean that a person is not capable of sinning. It takes faith to resist sin. That's one of the reasons it was given to us. The question is, are we using it to resist sin, or just to get "things"?

Now please don't misunderstand me, I am not advocating going back over to the other extreme and majoring on sin. But I am advocating a more realistic, and a more spiritual, understanding of this thing called sin.

There have been a lot of new believers added to the Church during the past ten or twelve years. And that is good. But the truth is, many of these new converts don't know the first thing about how to resist sin. All they have heard is how to get things from God, how to make positive affirmations, how to "confess" for this or that *thing*. All of that has its place. But it is not the Full Gospel. It is only one aspect of it.

Jesus did speak a great deal about faith. And faith is the instrument by which we receive all the good things which God wants to bestow upon His beloved children. But our Lord also had a good deal to say about living the Christian life. And one aspect of living the Christian life concerns overcoming sin. Unfortunately, most new Christians, especially in the faith movement, know all about faith for things, yet few have taken the time to teach them how to get sin out of their lives.

Does that mean that I am preaching *against* faith? No, I am not. I am a faith teacher—and a good one. Why would I want to teach against the very thing I am called to propagate?

I am not teaching against faith. What I am preaching against are the false notions and deceit that have arisen in some of our faith camps. God expects us to be strong in faith, but He does not expect us to compromise holiness in the process of developing our faith.

Genuine Repentance

True repentance is based upon conviction of sin. But there is a big difference between *conviction* and *condemnation*.

God is not a condemner. When you sin, God will never condemn you for it. He will never get on your back and tell you how ugly you are because you sin. Nor will He take away your car or home or children. He will not kill you, or break up your marriage or destroy your job or business.

Now the devil might do that. Because the Bible tells us that it is his nature: **The thief** (Satan) **cometh not, but for to steal, and to kill, and to destroy....**(John 10:10a). Satan will also put you under condemnation for your sin. The Bible calls him the accuser of the brethren. (Rev. 12:10.) As someone has pointed out, the devil will tempt you into sinning, and then immediately condemn you for doing it!

But not God. James tells us, **Let no man say when he is tempted, I am tempted of God: for God cannot be tempted with evil, neither tempteth he any man** (James 1:13). And Paul assures us, **There is therefore now no condemnation to them which are in Christ Jesus, who walk not after the flesh, but after the Spirit** (Rom. 8:1)

But God will convict of sin. Conviction is laid on a person's heart for no other reason than to lead him to a godly sorrow. And the Bible says that **godly sorrow worketh repentance** (2 Cor. 7:10). But repentance does not mean apologizing to God:

"I'm sorry God; forgive me."

"I forgive you."

"Oh, I did it again, I'm sorry. I just can't help doing that."

That is not repentance. When a person genuinely repents, he goes before

God with a godly *sorrow* in his heart, almost ashamed of himself. He bows his knee before the Most High God and says: "Lord, I have sinned. I ask You to forgive me. I will never do it again." Then he turns his back on his sin and fights against it with every bit of faith he has in him.

That is true repentance.

Conditioned to Sin

Then the Lord showed me that there was a need of repentance in my own life. He revealed to me that there were some things in my life that I had not cleaned up, things I had just accepted. Oh, it wasn't a question of forgiveness. I knew that God would forgive me of them. But that was part of the problem.

You see, I had such an assurance of God's forgiving nature that sin was no longer a despiteful thing to me. I would commit some sin, and immediately feel bad about it. But I knew I could get forgiveness of it. So then I would go along and at the first sign of temptation, I would fall right back into that same sin. The problem was not with God's forgiving nature, it was with my careless nature. I had allowed myself to become conditioned to sin.

Becoming conditioned to sin is always a dangerous thing for a Christian. Because it can happen so casually you almost aren't even aware it is taking place.

For example, you can sit and watch television for so long you finally get conditioned to accept adultery without a qualm. Now you may never commit it yourself. But if you sit and watch it long enough, it finally gets to where it doesn't look so bad to you any more. It begins to lose its abhorrence. It gradually becomes "acceptable."

That is one of the devil's favorite ruses. He works hard and strong to condition people to accept sin, to lull them into a false sense of security. He disguises his most vile practices and attitudes as "harmless entertainment."

One evening I was sitting and watching television. It was one of those typical commercial network "sit-coms" — situation comedies. Suddenly the Spirit of God spoke to me.

"Do you know what you are watching?" He asked.

"Yes Sir," I acknowledged, thinking He was speaking literally.

"Let Me show you what the devil has done," the Lord responded.

"What has he done?" I asked, not quite sure I understood what He was getting at.

"You aren't watching television," the Lord explained. "You are watching adultery, fornication, perversion — filth."

I got the message. I knew what He was referring to. Yet not once did that show mention any of those things by name. In fact, the whole show was funny; it was a comedy. And I like comedy.

Now I am a funny person; I'm really quite comical. I have a great sense of humor. I enjoy making people laugh and I like to laugh. So if something is funny, then I will usually sit and watch it. That's what I was doing this particular evening . . . I thought.

You see, the first time I sat and watched that show, it was repulsive to me. It turned me off, so I turned it off. Although it was the usual network fare, it was downright sinful. And I recognized it as such.

But the next time it came on, I watched it a little bit longer before switching it off. Then by the third time it came on, it didn't seem quite so bad, so I watched more of it. Finally, it got to where it didn't seem bad at all. It was funny. So I left it on. The next thing I knew, it had become a regular viewing habit. Yet the show had not really changed its basic nature. I had changed. I had allowed myself to become conditioned to sin.

It is easy for us as Christians to become conditioned to accept things God is against. Satan has a way of making sin seem harmless, or at least "forgivable."

That's what had happened to me about certain things in my life that I had come to accept. They were not tremendously evil things — they just represented a compromise with evil. They were things I knew better than to do. I knew they were wrong, but I was at a point where it was easier to go along with them than to fight against them.

Then there came a time when God said, "I want you to start hating the works of the devil with the same intensity that you love Me." You find out real quick how much you really love God when you start hating the works of the devil.

There are some things I dearly despise. I hate to see a person tormented by demons. I hate to see people destroyed by alcohol, or drugs, or adultery, or any other of the devil's devices. I hate Satan and everything he stands for. But if I hated him so much, why was I dabbling around in his territory?

We Christians must realize what it is we are playing around with when we adopt an easy attitude toward sin. There is a demon at large in this world of ours. He is trying his best to destroy lives — ours and those around us. And we have the power of God to stop him. There is going to come a time when we will see people who are tormented and bound up and possessed, and it will become so repulsive to us that we won't tolerate it anymore. We will step in and drive out that foul demon in the Name of Jesus.

But we will neither be prepared nor disposed to do that as long as we ourselves are bound by (or even playing around with) the same evil spirit. We must rid ourselves of our own sin if we are ever to help others to rid themselves of theirs.

The Lord said to me, "I have prophesied that I will build My Church and the gates of hell shall not prevail against it. I am now building that overcoming Church. As I build it, I am cleansing it so that nothing can stand against it."

We are the Church of which the Lord was speaking. And He has called that

Church glorious. (Eph. 5:27.) He says that every member, every part of His glorious Church, has been predestined to be conformed to the image of His own dear Son, Jesus Christ. (Rom. 8:29.)

What do you think the Lord Jesus thinks about sin? What is His attitude toward the works of the devil?

According to 1 John 3:8: **He that committeth sin is of the devil; for the devil sinneth from the beginning. For this purpose the Son of God was manifested, that he might destroy the works of the devil.**

Jesus came to this earth to destroy the works of Satan. As Jesus' disciples, that ought to be our calling. We ought to accept that calling and power to destroy the works of the devil, beginning first in our own lives. Then we will be cleansed and prepared to destroy his evil works in the lives of others.

2

Choose Whom You Will Serve

God gave me this message and told me to deliver it to His people. He instructed me to entitle it: *Choose You This Day Whom Ye Will Serve.*

That title contains a word that most Christians today seem to know very little about. I understand that there are some mature Christians to whom this message will not be particularly new because they have already come through what I am speaking of and are going on toward perfection in Christ. But generally speaking, most of us don't know much about the word "serve." We don't hear much about serving God these days — we only hear about how to receive His blessings.

Now don't misunderstand. There are blessings in the Christian life. Many of them. But the blessings of God are laid up for those who faithfully serve Him, not for those who grab hold of some "get-blessed-quick" formula.

You cannot take one isolated principle of God's Word, negate all the other principles in it, and try to get that one to work for you. You can't go around confessing good things, all the time allowing sin in your life, and still expect that confession to produce good — either for yourself or for others. It just won't work. At least, not for very long.

We call ourselves "Word people." But many times I think we would be better termed "favorite word" people. Just listen to us:

"I like that verse over there in Philippians, **My God shall supply all your need according to his riches in glory by Christ Jesus** (Phil. 4:19). I believe that. I'm a Word person, a faith man, a believer. I believe God meets all my needs!"

Yet the same God who inspired that verse also said, **. . . choose you this day whom ye will serve** (Josh. 24:15).

The same God who inspired the Apostle Paul to write, **I can do all things through Christ which strengtheneth me** (Phil. 4:13), also said, **So then because thou art lukewarm, and neither cold nor hot, I will spue thee out of my mouth** (Rev. 3:16).

I believe what God wants right now is a group of "hot" Christians. Christians who won't accept sin, who won't tolerate the works of the devil, who won't compromise their faith or godliness or holiness.

We have got to learn about holiness. We must learn about serving God. We are not servants of this world, of sin, of the devil. No more than we are under the dominion of disease, or poverty, or failure or defeat. The Bible says, **The steps of a good man are ordered by the Lord: and he delighteth in his way** (Ps. 37:23). Our steps are ordered by the Lord; we are under His control.

Paul tells us, **Ye are bought with a price; be not ye the servants of men**

(1 Cor. 7:23). We are not subject to the world or to the world's system, that is true.

But neither are we our own masters. Just one chapter back, this same Paul wrote:

> What? know ye not that . . . ye are not your own?

> For ye are bought with a price: therefore glorify God in your body, and in your spirit, which are God's.

> **1 Corinthians 6:19,20**

As God's servants, we have no right to choose what *we* want to do. It is God Who orders our steps; He is in command of our lives. We ought to get up every morning and report for duty to our Commander-in-Chief!

Fear the Lord

> Now therefore fear the Lord, and serve him in sincerity and in truth . . . .

> **Joshua 24:14**

This is not a fear like you might have of snakes or airplanes or elevators or cancer. It does not refer to dread or terror. This is reverential fear. It is the kind of fear that causes you not to want to do anything to displease someone.

I have that kind of fear about some godly men with whom I associate. When Brother Kenneth Hagin invites me to come and preach with him, I have a desire to do exactly what he wants me to do — no more and no less. I don't want to be pushy or inconsiderate. I don't want to try to take over the meeting or to do anything that will jeopardize his ministry or decrease his estimation of me. So I walk in reverential fear.

Now by doing that, I am not putting the man on a pedestal and calling him deity or anything like that. I just don't want to displease him. I respect his person and his office.

I feel the same way about Kenneth Copeland. I have great respect for Brother Copeland. I appreciate his life and ministry, his dedication to the Gospel. He is a great inspiration to my life. There are times when he and I get together just to have fun. But there are other times when I become a servant to him. On those occasions, I would literally polish his shoes, because he brings good news. Like David of old, I respect and honor God's anointed.

There are times when Brother Copeland and I may be on the same platform. It may not be in either of our organizations, we might just be guests, or speakers in a meeting. As he and I sit together, many times people will treat us as equals. But I don't treat Brother Copeland as an equal, but as a superior. I become a servant to him. And there are times when he does that for me as well; he has respect for my office and my calling, as I do for his.

One day I was preaching and the anointing of God was on me so strongly I could hardly stand up. The next thing I knew Brother Copeland was helping me out of the auditorium, carrying my coat. When I got to a room backstage, I began to try to relax because the anointing was so powerful I found it difficult to move. Suddenly I realized that Brother Copeland had taken my shoes off and was massaging my feet. That is the kind of attitude God is looking for in His people, regardless of their station in life.

Have An Attitude of Servitude

I have that kind of attitude. That's not boasting, it's just honesty. I have it, not because I am so great, but because I know how great God is. Recognizing Who and what He is, I want to do the things that please Him, and to avoid those things that displease Him.

No matter how big you or your ministry may become, always strive to stay humble before the Lord. It will pay rich dividends. There is something about serving, about having an attitude of servitude, that sets a person apart.

Servitude to God is not demeaning, it's not drudgery. With the right attitude, it's uplifting; it's a joy. My job has its difficult moments, but as far as I'm concerned, I've got the easy part. All I have to do is hear from God and preach. All of those who work on my staff, those who stay behind and do the day-to-day work so I can travel, those who attend to all the endless details of the meetings so I can be free to minister — they are the real servants. Yet they are servants by choice. I didn't force a one of them to come to work for me. They wanted to do so. Because they have an attitude of servitude. And God will bless them for it.

You can't hold anyone back who has such an attitude. Sooner or later, that person will reap all the good which he has sown in others. Because the Apostle Paul tells us in Colossians 3:23,24:

> **And whatsoever ye do, do it heartily, as to the Lord, and not unto men;**

> **Knowing that of the Lord ye shall receive the reward of the inheritance: for ye serve the Lord Christ.**

Those people who serve me are not really serving Jerry Savelle. I am only the beneficiary of their service, I'm not the object of that service. What they do, they do "as to the Lord," and it is ultimately from Him that they will receive the "reward of the inheritance."

There is something about servitude that ennobles a person. We should never think of servitude as being "beneath" us. We should always remember: **Even . . . the Son of man came not to be ministered unto, but to minister, and to give his life a ransom for many** (Matt. 20:28). Our Lord Jesus had an attitude of servitude.

That is the kind of attitude God is asking His people to display toward Him today.

Be Loyal

God wants His people not only to serve Him, but also to serve one another. Some Christians think that because they are "free," they are beyond serving others. They act as though they think being free means they don't have to be loyal to anything. That is not so. There is no such thing as a "free spirit," totally unattached to anything.

Sometimes when people come out of some particular denomination in which there was a great deal of regimentation and get into the Full Gospel movement, they begin to think: "Now that I am free, I don't have to go to church anymore!" Instead of attending church to fellowship with other believers, they think they can stay home if they like and listen to cassette tapes and call that "worship."

Where did they ever get such an idea? The Word of God clearly states that we are not to forsake the assembling of ourselves together. (Heb. 10:25.) And that does not refer to gathering the family around a tape player! There is a time and place for that, but it is not to take the place of corporate worship in the house of God.

There are no lone wolves in the Church of Jesus Christ. We need each other, to be attached to one another. We need to fellowship with people of like precious faith, to draw from them and allow them to draw from us.

Some people have the mistaken idea that since they are free from doctrinal bondage, they don't have to teach Sunday school or Bible study anymore. That too is false. Paul writes that the man (or woman) of God is to be . . . **apt to teach** (2 Tim. 2:24). *The Amplified Bible* says, **. . . he must be a skilled and suitable teacher.** The more we learn, the more we are responsible for sharing with others.

To be free from one thing demands loyalty to another. If we have been made free from the powers of hell, it is so we can become loyal to heaven and all it stands for. In that sense, no Christian can ever say, "I am free." Each one of us still belongs to God. And God makes demands upon us. One of those demands is loyalty.

As Christians we are to be loyal to the Head of the Church, Jesus Christ. We are also to be loyal to the Body of the Church.

Respect Authority

Once I served as a pastor of a church for about six years. The church had a

Christian school with about 200 students, and occasionally I would go in and speak to the high school students.

I remember one time I was speaking on the subject of rebellion, because some of the students had been showing signs of a rebellious attitude. I was teaching on disobedience: what it is, what God has to say about it, the consequences of it. When I had finished my remarks, one young man raised his hand and asked me, "Brother Jerry, how old does a person have to get so nobody can tell him what to do anymore?"

"There is no such age," I told that young man. "You are always going to be under somebody's authority."

That statement is as true for adults as it is for young people. You and I are going to be under authority from now on. But I'll tell you what is thrilling about that statement — it's not negative!

When we are under God's authority, we are not under the authority of a tyrant or a dictator, a despot or an ogre who is out to destroy us. Our God is love, all love. Being under God's authority and serving Him leads to nothing but good.

I do not regret for a moment bowing my knee to the Lord Jesus Christ on February 11, 1969 at 3 a.m. Nor will I ever regret it. Since then the Lord has led me into 18 years of Adventures In Faith. I have no desire to turn back now — I have nothing to turn back to.

What did I have before? Sickness, disease, a marriage that was about to break up, a business that was failing, a car that wouldn't run, hatred for other people who in turn hated me — hell while I lived and hell when I died.

No, I have nothing to turn back to — but everything to look forward to! Because, like the Apostle Paul, I can say: **. . . I know whom I have believed, and am convinced that he is able . . . .** (2 Tim. 1:12 *NIV*). That's the Person you should want to be under the authority of, the One Who is able, **. . . able to make all grace abound to you, so that in all things**

at all times, having all that you need, you will abound in every good work (2 Cor. 9:8 NIV).

Seek the Provider, Not the Provision

Now therefore fear the Lord, and serve him in sincerity and in truth: and put away the gods which your fathers served on the other side of the flood, and in Egypt; and serve ye the Lord.

Joshua 24:14

Now you may be thinking, "I don't know why preachers talk so much about serving God. After all, I'm not serving Buddha. I'm following Jesus."

What about money? Are you "believing for money" right now?

"Well," you might say, "it's one thing to 'believe for money,' it's another thing to *serve* it."

Is it? When your thoughts are continually on something, you are already serving it — in your mind. Whatever

44

occupies your mind and your time, that is what you are serving.

One day some time back, the Lord appeared to me in my hotel room. One of the things He told me in that visit was this: "Son, tell My people to stop seeking provision and start seeking the Provider."

Do you know it is very easy in our Christian walk to get our attention on the wrong thing, even though that thing is good? When we begin to find out all that God wants us to have, all that we are entitled to as His dear children, it is sometimes hard to focus our attention on the Provider rather than on the provision.

The Psalmist said: . . . **those who seek the Lord lack no good thing** (Ps. 34:10 NIV). Notice the tense of this translation. If we are seeking the Lord, we already have everything we need — we lack no good thing.

The problem is we have learned so much about faith in the past few years that we have got our attention on our faith rather than on **the author and finisher of our faith** (Heb. 12:2). Now, we needed to know more about faith because we were ignorant of it. Ignorant of what it was and how to use it. Now that we know that, we need to learn what to use it for.

God never intended for us to use our faith just to accumulate all the things we are lusting after. God wants us to develop our faith so we can win this world to Him, to snatch people out of the jaws of hell. Faith wasn't given to us to provide full employment for those turning out all the goods and services we want. God gave us faith for the same reason He gave it to Jesus — to use to glorify the Father in heaven by doing always those things that please Him. (John 8:29.)

Like Jesus, we Christians are to be about our Father's business. And our Father is in the soulwinning business. He has promised that if we will attend to His business, He will attend to ours: **But seek ye first the kingdom of God, and his righteousness; and all these things shall be added unto you** (Matt. 6:33).

Serve God, Not Mammon

No man can serve two masters: for either he will hate the one, and love the other; or else he will hold to the one, and despise the other. Ye cannot serve God and mammon.

Therefore I say unto you, Take no thought for your life, what ye shall eat, or what ye shall drink; nor yet for your body, what ye shall put on. Is not the life more than meat, and the body than raiment?

Behold the fowls of the air: for they sow not, neither do they reap, nor gather into barns; yet your heavenly Father feedeth them. Are ye not much better than they? . . . .

Therefore take no thought, saying, What shall we eat? or, What shall we drink? or, Wherewithal shall we be clothed?

(For after all these things do the Gentiles seek:) for your heavenly Father knoweth that ye have need of all these things.

Matthew 6:24-26,31,32

Joshua 24:14 said: **Now therefore fear the Lord, and serve him in sincerity and**

in truth: and put away the gods which your fathers served . . . . In other words, you can't serve God and other gods. In Matthew 6:24 Jesus said the same thing: **No man can serve two masters . . . .**

But notice that right after He says that no man can serve two masters, He tells us to take no thought for our life, that God knows we need the necessities of life. In verse 33 He promises us that if we will center our thoughts on God rather than on things, He will see to it that we receive all the things we need.

We cannot serve two masters. We can't serve God and His provision. If we try to serve the provision, we are going to lose contact with the Provider. If we want to stay in fellowship with God, we must seek Him, not His gifts.

There are so many faith people who don't know one thing about fellowship with God. All they know is some formula for getting things. They have no idea what an intimate relationship with God is all about.

God never intended for a tape or a paperback book to take the place of our intimate fellowship with Him. Those things are just teaching aids. They just inspire us to go do what that fellow who wrote or recorded them did. But what God wants us to do is to come into personal and intimate contact with Him. He wants us to serve Him with sincerity of heart. We cannot serve God and things —as good as those things may be.

> **And if it seem evil to you to serve the Lord, choose you this day whom ye will serve . . . .**
>
> **Joshua 24:15**

Now God puts it very plainly: "Either you serve Me, or you serve some other god. If you've got it in your mind that serving Me is not good, then choose today whom you will serve."

God does not appreciate people who try to straddle the fence. God will not accept from His people a divided heart. (Hos. 10:2.) The Bible says that God is a spirit and those who worship Him must worship Him in spirit and in truth. (John 4:24.)

God is a jealous God. He will not share us with another god. No more than my wife will share me with another woman, or that I will share her with another man.

In essence, God says to us: "Choose this day whom you will serve. If you don't want any part of Me, that's fine. But you must choose. I will not accept a divided heart. You cannot run to Me when you are in trouble, and then run to someone (or something) else when things are going well. With Me, it's all or nothing."

God expects us to serve Him and not things. But He has also assured us that if we will serve Him and not things, He will pile up the things we need. When we are totally committed to God, He will see to it that we do not lack any good thing.

But we must get our priorities straight. Just because God has promised us some things doesn't mean that we should go seeking those things, that we should set as our goal the accumulation of things and leave the Provider out.

When you really enter into fellowship with God, all of the things of this world become very minor. Can you imagine five minutes with the Creator of the Universe? Can you imagine His talking to you as He would with a dear friend?

Perhaps you would consider it a great privilege to be able to sit down for five minutes with Kenneth Copeland. You might think it would be wonderful to be able to shake hands with Oral Roberts. Maybe you would give anything if the President of the United States would invite you to dinner at the White House.

Yet God is saying to you right now, "Come on up to the throne. Let's talk a little bit. There are some new things I want to do, but before I do them I want to discuss them with you personally." Does that interest you at all? Or are you just interested in showing God your "want list"?

Now I value the time I get to sit down and fellowship with Brother Copeland. I appreciate the time I got to shake Oral Roberts' hand. I haven't had dinner with the President yet, but I am sure I would be thrilled and honored if I had that privilege. But none of these things compares to one minute with Almighty God. Nothing on earth can compare to one minute of being swallowed up in His divine Presence.

David said of the Lord: **Thou wilt shew me the path of life: in thy presence is fulness of joy; at thy right hand there are pleasures for evermore** (Ps. 16:11).

There is nothing that can take the place of fellowship with the God of the Universe. Oh, the experiences we've missed out on because we haven't understood the marvelous privilege and joy that is ours in serving God! We've had such a distorted, negative image of serving our loving heavenly Father.

"Oh, the price you have to pay to serve God," people say. Yes, it is true that there is a price to pay. But the beautiful thing is, you can well afford it! Because

I can assure you, service to God *pays* a great deal more than it *costs*!

Despite what you may hear people say, it is not hard to serve God. The hard thing is serving the flesh, serving the world. Because as someone has said, "Money makes a wonderful servant, but a terrible master." That could be said of any of the things of the world. But thank God, He has given us dominion over this world and the things of it, so that we do not serve them — they serve us. We serve the Living God!

3

As For Me and My House, We Will Serve the Lord

**And if it seem evil unto you to serve
the Lord, choose you this day whom ye
will serve; whether the gods which your
fathers served that were on the other side
of the flood, or the gods of the Amorites,
in whose land ye dwell: but as for me
and my house, we will serve the Lord.**

Joshua 24:15

After giving the children of Israel a
choice of which gods they would serve,
Joshua spoke up real quickly to make
known his own personal decision: **But as
for me and my house, we will serve the
Lord.**

If you haven't made that decision yet,
you need to do it. And not just once.
Every time the devil comes to harass or
to tempt you, you should stomp your foot

and declare in no uncertain terms, "Devil, I'm not listening to you. I'm not following you any longer. I don't know about anyone else, but as for me and my house, we will serve the Lord!" You will never regret it.

Someone once sent me a little plaque which reads: *As for me and my house, we will serve the Lord.* I hung it on the wall of my study to remind me of Whose I am. Like the Roman Centurion, I am a man under authority. I'm not free to do as I please. I move by the direction of the Holy Spirit. Whatever God says to me, that's what I must do, regardless of what others may think or say or do.

Back in 1981 I had to make a hard decision. God began changing the direction of my life and ministry. At that time, He spoke to me through a verse in Romans in which Paul says in essence: "I am in debt to every man." (Rom. 1:14.) The Phillips translation says: "I feel myself under a sort of universal obligation . . . ."

When I read that verse the Spirit of God spoke to me and said, "You too are under universal obligation. Every man has a right to hear what you know."

Then He revealed to me what I was to do: "I am relieving you of the assignment I gave you six years ago to establish this church. Now you have a different assignment. You are to go tell the people of the church that you are going to merge it with another local body. You and your church are to become a part of it. I am doing this because I want you to be relieved of the responsibility of being a pastor so you will be free to go wherever I send you."

That's when I had to decide whether I was going to do what God said or not. It was not an easy decision to make. Ours was a very successful church, one capable of reaching the whole city for Christ. Yet I knew in my heart that God had spoken. What was I to do? What could I tell the people of that church, those who had worked so hard and so long to see it become a success?

So my wife and I went off to a cabin to pray about it for a couple of days.

While we were there the Lord spoke to me and said, "Go home and announce your decision to the church. And do it this Sunday morning."

"But, Lord," I protested, "that's pretty short notice."

"I don't need much notice," was His reply.

So early the next Sunday morning I went to call on the pastor of the church the Lord had spoken to me about.

"God told me to merge our church with yours," I told him. "He said that your congregation and ours are to become one. You are to be the leader of the church and I am to submit myself to you as my pastor."

The minister just grinned and replied, "Yes, I know. God showed me that in a dream last month."

That same Sunday morning I announced to our church that the Lord had spoken to me and what He had told me to do. I explained that I had already made the necessary arrangements with the pastor of the other church.

"Now tonight I am going over to that church," I told them, "and I'm inviting all of you to follow me over there. We are going to become a part of it."

That Sunday evening the pastor's people didn't know what was going on. He hadn't told them a thing. In the morning service he had just said, "You'd better be here tonight or you are going to miss seeing a miracle." They had no idea what he was talking about.

At six o'clock that big church was about a third full. By seven-thirty the ushers were having to bring in folding chairs to place in the aisles because of the overflow crowd. All of the people of that church were standing there looking, trying to figure out where all of these people were coming from. As I walked down the aisle, I could hear them whispering among themselves: "Isn't that Jerry Savelle? What's he doing here? Doesn't his church hold services on Sunday night?"

When the pastor and I stood up on the platform and announced the merger, the place went wild. Of course, as always, there were a few people who weren't in the flow. Because they didn't understand my decision, they got mad at me. Some called me up on the phone to complain, others wrote me nasty letters and made angry accusations. And it hurt. After all, I'm as human as anyone else. I don't like to be misunderstood, to be criticized and falsely accused. But I had made up my mind that I would rather hear God say, "Well done, good and faithful servant," than to have the praises of men.

Several years have passed since then, and now everyone is saying, "I'll tell you what, Brother Jerry, you were right when you made that decision back then." I'm glad to hear them say that. I appreciate it. But it really doesn't change anything. Whether I was right or wrong is not the point; the important thing is, was I obedient to the voice of God? That's really all that matters. And that's what should matter to you too — being obedient to the Lord.

Sometimes being obedient, serving the Lord, means turning around right in the middle of the stream and going in the opposite direction. If that's what God says to do, do it! As Christians, we are people under authority. God is our Commander-in-Chief; He makes the decisions. The Lord orders our steps; all He wants us to do is to follow. To follow the Lord may go against the grain of our theology, but we must be willing to lay down our theology and serve God.

We Will Serve the Lord

And the people answered and said, God forbid that we should forsake the Lord, to serve other gods;

For the Lord our God, he it is that brought us up and our fathers out of the land of Egypt, from the house of bondage, and which did those great signs in our sight, and preserved us in all the way wherein we went, and among all the people through whom we passed:

And the Lord drave out from before us all the people, even the Amorites which dwelt in the land: therefore will we also serve the Lord; for he is our God.

And Joshua said unto the people, Ye cannot serve the Lord: for he is an holy God; he is a jealous God; he will not forgive your transgressions nor your sins.

If ye forsake the Lord, and serve strange gods, then he will turn and do you hurt, and consume you, after that he hath done you good.

And the people said unto Joshua, Nay; but we will serve the Lord.

And Joshua said unto the people, Ye are witnesses against yourselves that ye have chosen you the Lord, to serve him. And they said, We are witnesses.

Now therefore put away, said he, the strange gods which are among you, and incline your heart unto the Lord God of Israel.

And the people said unto Joshua, The Lord our God will we serve, and his voice will we obey.

Joshua 24:16-24

This passage is found in the last chapter of the Book of Joshua. In the first chapter of the next book, Judges, we find this verse:

> **Now after the death of Joshua it came to pass, that the children of Israel asked the Lord, saying, Who shall go up for us against the Canaanites first, to fight against them?**

> **Judges 1:1**

Notice that back in Joshua, chapter 24, they had said, "We will serve the Lord." Then as soon as Joshua dies, they ask, "Who is going to lead us?" They seemed to forget so quickly Whom it was they were supposed to be following and serving.

By the second chapter of Judges they had run into problems and come under pressure:

> **And the children of Israel did evil in the sight of the Lord, and served Baalim:**

> **And they forsook the Lord God of their fathers, which brought them out of the land of Egypt, and followed other gods, of the gods of the people that were round about them, and bowed themselves unto them, and provoked the Lord to anger.**

And they forsook the Lord, and served Baal and Ashtaroth.

And the anger of the Lord was hot against Israel, and he delivered them into the hands of spoilers that spoiled them, and he sold them into the hands of their enemies round about, so that they could not any longer stand before their enemies.

Whithersoever they went out, the hand of the Lord was against them for evil, as the Lord had said, and as the Lord had sworn unto them: and they were greatly distressed.

Nevertheless the Lord raised up judges, which delivered them out of the hand of those that spoiled them.

And yet they would not hearken unto their judges, but they went a whoring after other gods, and bowed themselves unto them: they turned quickly out of the way which their fathers walked in, obeying the commandments of the Lord; but they did not so.

Judges 2:11-17

As Christians, all of us made a decision to serve God. There came a time in each of our lives when we individually and personally realized our need of God. My time was February 11, 1969. It was then that I realized my need for Jesus. At the moment I said, "Jesus, You are my Lord," I did what Joshua told these people to do. I chose that day whom I would serve.

Since that time, I have been faced with "other gods" — things which have come into my life to draw my attention away from the Lord. Although I have always remained true to God and would never serve the devil again, still there have been things which could have distracted me from serving Him — if I had allowed them to do so.

When a person is in a growing ministry such as mine, when he begins to gain some exposure and some measure of wealth or fame or power, it is very easy to start desiring all of those things and not serve God properly.

When a person in my position begins to realize all that is available to him, it is very easy to allow those things to creep into his life and displace his commitment and devotion to God alone. If he is not constantly on his guard, before he even realizes it, everything he is doing has become centered on his ability and his activity rather than on his Source. If he is not careful, he begins to try to build a ministry instead of being content to serve God.

One time I had to stop and ask myself, "Jerry Savelle, why are you doing all this? What is really in your heart? Do you have a genuine love for people, or do you just want to be a big-name evangelist?"

I was so troubled I got before the Lord and opened my spirit up to Him.

The Lord began to "try my reins and my heart," as the Bible says in Psalm 26:2. And He found some things there that were not pleasing to Him.

As He would hold them up, one by one, before my spiritual eye, He would say, "Get that out." And I would do so. But it was like pulling teeth — it hurt.

Some I really had to wrestle with. I would say, "Oh, God, let's go on to the next one and come back to this one later."

"No," He would say. "We're not going any further until you have dealt with this one."

So, one by one, I got those things out of my life and found true freedom and release. When I was through, I never felt so good in all of my life.

And then there were some things that I thought perhaps I was lacking in. But God said, "No, you're doing fine there." I wasn't all wrong, just as you are not all wrong. There are some things in your life about which you are very sure, sincere and dedicated. There may be some other things about which you need to make some hard decisions. If you will open yourself up to God, He will show you which is which and tell you what to do about them, just as He did with me.

God is saying to us, "I'm not condemning you. I'm not out to harm you or hurt you. I just want to help you."

God loves us. He is trying to tell us, "Don't do what the children of Israel did. Don't choose Me and then allow 'other gods' to influence you, to drag you back into bondage and destruction."

You see, there are a lot of people who don't want to serve God, but they want the benefits of serving God. People have actually told me, "I can't do what you are talking about, but, dear me, I need those blessings! Agree with me that all of God's blessings will come upon me."

I can't agree with people that all of God's blessings will come upon them unless they are willing to hearken diligently unto the voice of the Lord their God.

God is saying to us today: "Wake up, Church! Shake yourself out of your lethargy! Examine yourself! Who are you serving? What are you serving? Are you serving the provisions or the Provider? Are you serving My blessings or are you serving Me? My blessings belong to you. My provisions belong to you. No devil in hell can keep them from you, *if* you will totally consecrate and dedicate yourself to Me. I will give them to you, I will lavish them upon you; but first I must have YOU!

"Choose you this day Whom ye will serve!"

4

Don't Get Satisfied

There are many satisfied Christians sitting in churches all over the country today. Nothing at all is happening in their churches, and that's just the way they like it. If anybody with the least bit of unction comes in, it creates waves. And they don't like waves. They get a little bit disturbed about getting disturbed: "It has taken us ten years to get things just like we like them; don't start rocking the boat!"

That's not the way God operates. Our God is never satisfied with the status quo. He is always on the move, always stretching our horizons. God does not want us satisfied with the level of our spiritual maturity.

I believe there is always something more out there to reach for, an anointing that we have not yet stepped into. I believe there are greater heights to scale, greater accomplishments to attain than we have even imagined. And I don't intend to quit until I see them manifested.

I will never be satisfied until every person I pray for is instantly healed, until every wheelchair victim gets up and walks.

With What You've Done

There is nothing that can compare with seeing God's miracle power at work right before your very eyes.

One time in one of my crusades there was a little brain-damaged seven-year-old girl who had the mentality level of an infant. Her mother had brought her to the service in her arms. She had no control over her nervous system at all. She was like a vegetable. All she could do was groan, a groaning that grieved your heart.

That little girl looked so lifeless as she sat on the front pew next to her mother. She was so pitiful looking, I had to be very careful not to allow myself to get into sympathy. Because sympathy looks at the problem and says, "My soul, I wish there were something I could do." But compassion says, "Do it!"

Jesus was never moved by sympathy; He was always moved by compassion. Compassion looks at a case like this and says, "My Father can fix that!" Sometimes the things that compassion commands you to do are, in the eyes of some people, cruel and hard. But when they are done in the flow of the Spirit of God, they will bring results. So I had to watch myself with that child, I had to keep myself from getting into sympathy with her.

So I began to preach, and the more I preached the more the anointing of God began to come upon me. All of a sudden that case didn't look so impossible anymore. That disease didn't look incurable any longer.

The Bible says that faith comes by hearing, and hearing by the Word of God. (Rom. 10:17.) I was hearing myself preach the Word of God, and so faith came. (Sometimes preachers can preach themselves right into faith.)

Suddenly the Spirit of God spoke up on the inside of me and said: "Pick up that child. Carry her in your arms while you preach and My anointing will flow into her body."

So I did as I was told. I took that child and just wrapped my arms around her. I held her up close to me and carried her all over the auditorium as I preached. She was moaning and her legs were hanging lifeless, her head was bobbing, and to the people I know it was a repulsive sight. I'm sure they must have thought, "What a jerk! What is the matter with that idiot? What does he think he is doing?"

But the anointing of God began to flow. In a few minutes the Spirit of God said to me: "Now give the child back to her mother and tell her to take her home; before morning there will be a drastic change."

So I handed the child back to the mother and gave her God's message. Then I went on with my sermon.

The next day that woman came running into the auditorium shouting, "Let me tell you what happened to my baby!" And she told us her story.

The parents kept the girl in a crib with rails on it so she wouldn't fall out. During the night they heard a noise in her bedroom, so they ran to see what had happened. The girl was not in her bed, she had climbed out and was sitting on the floor. When they switched on the lights, she looked up at them and said, "Mama?" That was the first word she had ever spoken in her life!

That morning the parents set their little girl up at the table with them instead of in the high chair in which they usually spoon-fed her like a baby. For the first time in seven years, that child fed herself!

Now there is no greater joy in the world than that. And I'll never be satisfied until every such child is made completely whole.

With What You Know

The worst thing we Christians can do is to get satisfied with what we know right now about God's Word. It is that same Word which set us free from sin and hell that sets us free from *all* the power of Satan. It is the same Word that we are to learn to use to set others free. Until we truly learn that, we haven't even begun to learn. Until we learn why we have been redeemed, what we have been set free to accomplish in life, we really know nothing of life at all.

In his letter to the Philippians the Apostle Paul spoke of this very thing:

> . . . I consider everything a loss compared to the surpassing greatness of knowing Christ Jesus my Lord, for whose sake I have lost all things . . . .
>
> I want to know Christ and the power of his resurrection . . . .
>
> Not that I have already obtained all this, or have already been made perfect, but I press on to take hold of that for which Christ Jesus took hold of me . . . .
>
> All of us who are mature should take such a view of things . . . .
>
> Philippians 3:8,10,12,15 NIV

What is your view of "things"? Are they your reason for being, the focus of your life, the object of your faith? Are you primarily interested in things, or in knowledge?

The deeper I get into the Word of God, the more I realize what Paul meant when he said that the greatest quest of his life was to know Christ, to take hold of that for which Christ had taken hold of him. That knowledge is the key to truly mature, successful Christian living.

Like Paul, I know Whom I have believed. But also like him, I am not content with the knowledge I have of Him. I want more. And the more I get, the more I want. I know more now than I did when I first came to Christ, but I don't know yet all that I intend to know about Him. As Paul says, all of us who are mature should take such a view.

We must not allow ourselves to become satisfied with what we have learned about our God. We cannot put God in a box and say, "Well, this is how

He worked in 1949, so that's how He will work today." No, God is bigger than that. He won't be kept in a box. He is a diversified character. Our God is a God of newness, of freshness. He springs things on us. Just when we think we know all there is to know about Him and His ways, He surprises us with some totally new and unsuspected facet of His personality.

I get both amused and grieved at the same time when I hear people say, "Well, I'm not going to listen to this faith teaching anymore, I know all there is to know about all that."

The only thing such a statement as that proves is just the opposite, that the person who made it doesn't know anything about faith. If he knew anything, he would know better than to make such a statement.

Listen to what the great Apostle Paul, writer of two-thirds of the New Testament, had to say on this subject:

> **Brothers, I do not consider myself yet to have taken hold of it.**
>
> **Philippians 3:13 NIV**

None of us has arrived yet. None of us knows all there is to know about anything, much less about the inexhaustible Word of God. Not even a part of it. We could spend an eternity just digging up the nuggets in Mark 11:23 alone.

We must not allow ourselves to get satisfied with what we have learned or what we have seen. We must keep striving for more.

God has impressed upon my spirit that many of His people have backslidden. They are lying out there somewhere wounded and hurt. For one reason or another, they are no longer fellowshipping with other Christians, are no longer involved in the things of God.

"My heart cries for them," the Lord told me. "I want revival to come to those poor hurting, bleeding people. Don't let them go."

Any person who claims that he has learned all he needs to know about faith, has missed the most basic principle of it: What we have been given faith for.

As long as people are in need of God's healing, forgiving touch, we must not become satisfied with what we know.

With Where You Are

There are millions of people who have come into the knowledge of God but for some reason have backslidden or turned away from Him. Perhaps they were hurt by some preacher, or some congregation, or even some individual Christian. Now those people are hurting and are crying out for help. God says, "I want them back."

The reason some of them got hurt and wounded is because we became satisfied. God does not want us to have divided hearts. We can't serve pleasures and still serve the Provider. We cannot serve God and mammon. If we try, we are destined for a fall. Jesus taught that **if a house be divided against itself, that house cannot stand** (Mark 3:25).

We cannot allow ourselves to have one foot in heaven and one foot in the world;

there is no stability in such a stance. We must choose whom we will serve, either God or mammon. We can't serve both.

God does not want servitude in word only, He wants it to be with sincerity and with truth. If we are going to serve the Lord wholeheartedly, then we must quit fooling around with the things of the world. We must take our stance for God or against Him, and we must do it today. The Bible says, **. . . behold, now is the accepted time; behold, now is the day of salvation** (2 Cor. 6:2).

Even people who are saved, who have come into a relationship with God, sometimes get snagged and conditioned by the things of the world. They say, "Well, I know this isn't of God, but it's all right. It's no big deal; God will understand." They begin to rationalize. They start straddling the fence. God warns us about adopting such an attitude: **So then because thou art lukewarm, and neither cold nor hot, I will spue thee out of my mouth** (Rev. 3:16).

God does not want lukewarm people, He wants us flaming with fire.

With Who You Are

When society has lowered its standards, it is very easy for the Church to do the same. In today's society anything goes. No one is concerned about perversion anymore. In fact, it has become the "in thing" not only to admit to, but actually to take pride in how perverted one is.

All kinds of sick people get on television and tell everybody how perverted they are. Of course, that's not what they call it, to them they are "liberated." It is the fad for such "liberated" ones to get together and form little special interest groups to "fight for their rights." They demand that the government protect and even subsidize their particular brand of perversion. And anyone who dares to raise his voice in protest is quickly branded a chauvinist, or worse.

Homosexuals, lesbians, prostitutes, abortionists, sexists, witches, atheists, cultists of every kind and sort are all taking up their banners and taking to the streets in an effort to draw attention to themselves and to their "cause." They all like the word "minority" because that sets them apart, it identifies them as "the few, the proud, the persecuted."

If such people would ever get turned on to God, they would soon discover that in His sight there is no such thing as a minority. He is no respecter of persons. (Acts 10:34.) God is an "equal opportunity" Redeemer.

The problem is, most of our society doesn't want to be redeemed, they want to be "recognized" — recognized and approved for what they are, as they are. Unfortunately, as loving and forgiving as He is, God cannot save the "righteous." He only calls sinners to repentance.

Until a person recognizes and acknowledges his need of God's forgiveness, he can never receive it — though it is freely available to him. So as long as society claims there is nothing wrong with them or their lifestyle, God cannot give them real life — eternal life, life in all its abundance.

But the sad thing about that kind of attitude is that it has crept into the Church. Instead of taking the Church to the world, Christians have brought the world into the Church. We have lowered our standards to those of society. We have adopted their humanistic philosophy of "respecting everyone's right to be himself," which sounds reasonable, even noble, until it is examined closely.

Upon closer inspection, it really means nothing less than granting everyone license to live any way he pleases. And we have fallen for that ruse. By accepting the world "as they are," we have come to accept ourselves "as we are."

We have become satisfied with who we are and how we are. And that is always a danger for the Church of Jesus Christ.

With What You Are Doing

More born-again, Spirit-filled Christians, so-called Word people, are getting divorces right now than ever before in the history of the Church. Instead of living up to God's standard for their lives, they have adopted the world's standard. The Word says, **What therefore God hath joined together, let not man put asunder** (Matt. 19:6). The world says, "If two people can't live together in harmony, let them get a divorce." There are many Christians who have fallen for this deception.

I know some Christian people right now who, from all appearances, are strong in the Word, even preaching the Gospel. Yet they have decided they wanted someone else besides their spouse. They have become so deceived by the world's way of thinking, they actually believe they can leave their mate and go live with someone else and that God will bless that arrangement. They go around confessing, "We are blessed . . . We are blessed . . ." all the while living in open adultery.

God has no choice; He must turn His back on such trash. When the Church starts lowering its standard to that of society, we are in trouble.

Hasn't God told us: **But you are a chosen people, a royal priesthood, a holy nation, a people belonging to God, that you may declare the praises of him who called you out of darkness into his wonderful light** (1 Pet. 2:9 NIV)?

How can we declare the praises of God Who has called us out of darkness into light, if we are still living in the same darkness as the world? How are we going to win the world if we lower our standards to theirs? We tell them that sin is wrong, and then join them in it. No wonder the world perceives us Christians as compromisers, or worse, as hypocrites.

God said that we are to choose whom we will serve. We cannot serve as a light to the world as long as we are doing the same things they are doing. We must not be satisfied to live in darkness.

With Your Service to God

We have taken God too lightly. We play with His love.

"God loves us," we mouth, attempting to justify ourselves. "We can do anything we want and God will still love us."

That may be true, but it is not the attitude God wants out of His people. I think we Christians sometimes unconsciously try to push God just to see how far we can go, how much we can get away with. Have your children ever done that to you? You gave them some liberty and they abused it? They pushed and pushed and pushed until you finally had to "lay down the law"?

That is a good phrase, because that is exactly what God is doing right now. God is "laying down the law" to us Christians. He is saying to us: "There is a mighty outpouring of My Spirit on the way. It is going to come upon the earth like a flood. Either My people are going to get in it and ride the crest of it, or they are going to be swept under by it."

87

God doesn't have time to play around with us anymore. And we can't play around with Him. We can't engage in religious games. We can't go through the Bible anymore and find the scriptures we like, and keep passing over those that make demands upon us.

The same self-centered attitude that the world has, is being brought into the Church. The only reason some people ever study the Bible, their only motivation for learning anything about faith, is just to try to get some of the "things" they are lusting after. If that is your motive for studying the Word of God, you should know it is not pleasing to Him.

God wants us in His Word so we can know Him. In fact, the very first reason for our having faith is not so we can have things, but so we can please God. So we can declare the praises of Him Who called us out of darkness into His wonderful light. And pleasing God has its rewards. Solomon tells us: **When a man's ways please the Lord, he maketh even his enemies to be at peace with him** (Prov. 16:7).

I don't want to leave the impression that God does not want us to believe for the things we need. He does. But when that becomes our only motive, it is not pleasing to Him.

I served as pastor of a church for six years. During that time I counseled many people who had no idea what a relationship with God was all about. All they wanted was a formula to get things. Some kind of "get-rich-quick" scheme. There are no such things in the Bible. God doesn't have any formulas for us to run through our little computer to get rich overnight.

(I would suggest that if anyone offers you some kind of formula like that, you'd better check it out very carefully. It is probably illegal.)

God doesn't have a formula, He has a lifestyle. He says that if you and I will adopt that lifestyle and live by it, eventually it will produce fruit — the fruit of righteous living.

Don't ever become satisfied with anything less than that.

5

Give Your Heart to God

And if it seem evil unto you to serve
the Lord, choose you this day whom ye
will serve; whether the gods which your
fathers served that were on the other side
of the flood, or the gods of the Amorites,
in whose land ye dwell: but as for me
and my house, we will serve the Lord.

And the people answered and said,
God forbid that we should forsake the
Lord, to serve other gods.

Joshua 24:15,16

There are many people who wouldn't
say with their mouth, "Oh, I am forsak-
ing the Lord." But in their hearts they
have done just that. As we have seen, just
a few verses after this passage, after the
death of Joshua, the children of Israel
began to conform to the inhabitants of the
land of Canaan. They began to adopt the
way of thinking of the Canaanites, to

conform to the society of their day. They made a confession of fidelity to God with their mouth, but they were not faithful in their heart.

Have you ever heard the expression, "Talk is cheap"? God wants more than our talk. He wants our heart.

Do you remember when God made His covenant with Abraham? He said that the token of their covenant agreement would be circumcision. That cutting of the flesh served as a sign to Abraham that he was a covenant man. As far as Abraham was concerned, he had no choice as to Whom he would serve; he belonged to Almighty God. He carried a token, a mark, of that covenant in his flesh. (Gen. 17.)

You and I don't have to experience circumcision of the flesh today, the Bible says that we are circumcised in the heart:

> For he is not a Jew, which is one outwardly; neither is that circumcision, which is outward in the flesh:

**But he is a Jew, which is one
inwardly; and circumcision is that of the
heart, in the spirit, and not in the letter;
whose praise is not of men, but of God.**

Romans 2:28,29

I like what the Apostle Paul said in
Galatians 6:17: **From henceforth let no
man trouble me: for I bear in my body
the marks of the Lord Jesus Christ.** Paul
carried in his physical body evidence of
the persecution he had suffered for Jesus'
Name. But more than that he had the
marks of circumcision in his heart.

That's what he was referring to when
he said in verse 14 of that same chapter:
**But God forbid that I should glory, save
in the cross of our Lord Jesus Christ, by
whom the world is crucified unto me,
and I unto the world.** In other words, he
was saying that because his heart had
been circumcised, the world no longer
had any attraction for him, any hold on
him. He was a love slave to Jesus Christ.

That's what we are to be.

> And the people answered and said,
> God forbid that we should forsake the
> Lord, to serve other gods;
>
> For the Lord our God, he it is that
> brought us up and our fathers out of the
> land of Egypt, from the house of bon-
> dage . . . .

Joshua 24:16,17a

Some people serve God only because
of some good thing He might do for
them. I wonder how many people would
serve God today if He were to announce:
"I want you to serve Me, but henceforth
I am discontinuing all blessings."

I'm afraid if God made such an
announcement as that, the result would
be like Gideon's army of ten thousand
who were put to the test to cull out those
who were afraid or unfit for duty. (Judges
7:1-7.) God would look around and there
would be about 300 left!

Why am I serving God? Because of
His blessings? No. I am serving God
because I love Him. I will serve Him all
my days whether He ever does anything
for me or not.

If God didn't do anything for us at all but cause us to escape an eternity in hell, that is reason enough to shout for glory! But the truth is, that's not all He can and will do for us — both in this life and in the life to come.

Yes, God has promised to make us the head and not the tail, above and not beneath, to bless us coming in and going out, to bless us in the city and in the field. Yes, God has promised to give us a surplus of prosperity and abundant life. Yes, God has promised that we will reign with Him as kings and priests. All that is true. And marvelous.

But what God needs right now is a people who would serve Him even if they never had a one of those promises. A people who love Him so much they are determined to be obedient and faithful to Him if they *never* see a better car, or a better home, or more money. That's the kind of people God is looking for. God wants sincerity of heart.

Check Your Motives

The reason I know about all this is because at one time in my life I had to check my own motives for serving the Lord. I had to bow down before Him and ask Him to forgive me of some wrong motives, for getting my eyes on things instead of on Him. I had to decide whether I was going to continue to serve the Lord whether those things ever came or not.

Some time ago I was going through a period of fasting and prayer. I wanted God to examine my heart. My prayer was that of the Psalmist David: **Examine me, O Lord, and prove me; try my reins and my heart** (Ps. 26:2).

Actually I knew He was well aware of what was there, but I wanted to know myself, to be sure for myself that my motives were pure and right. I knew that the New Testament says: **Examine yourselves, whether ye be in the faith; prove your own selves** (2 Cor. 13:5a). I remembered that 1 Corinthians 2:11a says,

For what man knoweth the things of a man, save the spirit of man which is in him?

So I went up to a cabin and got before the Lord. I cried out: "Father, I want You to help me to search my heart and check my motives. I'm going to lay everything before You. Show me the truth."

God had been dealing with me about certain things for several months. I would face those things and attempt to approach them with the Word, but there was something that had me puzzled. And I needed desperately to get it settled.

You see, God had blessed me greatly. He had blessed me with things. My wife, Carolyn, and I have always been liberal with the things with which the Lord has blessed us. We don't let things stick to us or possess us. I've been blessed in being able to give away cars, airplanes, money and things like that. When we feel that something is beginning to possess us, that's when we take authority over it and give it away.

I never know when I get home if I am going to have any furniture or not. My wife is likely to have given it all away. She has been known to do that on occasion. It doesn't matter if we just bought it and it is still in the box, if the Spirit of God moves on her to give it to some young couple just starting out, or someone else who needs it more than we do — out it goes!

There have been times when I have come home and didn't have a bed to sleep in. But then the next time I'd come home, we'd have a new one. God has always supplied. We've been that way with the things that God has blessed us with. We've been givers, we love to give.

But there were some things that God had blessed me with that I didn't even have the time to use. They just seemed to be piling up, gathering dust. And it bothered me.

God Knows Your Heart

After one meeting in Oklahoma, my dad and my pilot came to pick me up in my private plane. As we were flying back to Fort Worth, Dad turned to me and said, "Boy, you ought to see what the Lord gave you while you were gone."

"What did He give me this time?" I asked.

"Well," he replied, "a fellow came over today and said he has been a partner in your ministry for a number of years and has been blessed by it. He said, 'I have always supported Jerry's ministry, but I've never done anything for him personally. So I thought it was time I did.' "

"Is that right?"

"Yeah, and you know what he did? He bought a brand new gold-wing Honda motorcycle and told me, 'Give this to Jerry; tell him to have fun.' "

"Are you kidding me?" I asked surprised.

"No, it's sitting at your house right now."

So when we got home that night I opened the garage door and there sat one of the most beautiful motorcycles I have ever seen. I would never have bought anything like that on my own. I had probably only ridden a motorcycle about three times in the past 14 years — and all three times it was fun. But I would never have gone out and bought a motorcycle for myself. There are too many other things I need worse than a motorcycle. Still, I must admit that I love to ride one. So naturally I was pleased and excited.

I could hardly wait until the next day to get on that thing. I got up early the next morning and rode it all around the neighborhood. I lived out in the country where there were a lot of winding roads, so I went all around the lake riding my new motorcycle. And as I rode along in the quietness and stillness of early morning, the peace of God came all over me. It was like a breath of fresh air.

Unless you travel constantly as I do, you may not realize what it is like to be on the go 24 hours a day, living out of hotel rooms and eating restaurant food. It is not as glamorous as it may appear. In fact, it gets tiresome.

Now I wouldn't trade jobs with anyone in the world, but sometimes I have to use my faith to stay in some of the hotels I'm put up in and eat in some of the places I do. When I pray over a meal, it's not just because it's the "religious" thing to do. I say something like this:

"Father, You said that those who believe in You would not be hurt if they drank any deadly thing; now Lord, for this I am about to receive make me truly *immune!*"

Now, don't misunderstand me, I love my work. If I am home too long at a time, I am like a lion in a cage. I have to get out on the road again, out where the people are. That's my calling, my ministry. But when you spend 95 percent of your life on the road, as I do, it does get old!

After I have been gone from home for three or four weeks at a time, all I can think of is getting back home to a good home-cooked meal. Of course, the family has been eating nothing but home-cooked meals all this time, so they are looking forward to my return so we can all go out to eat. There are sacrifices to be made to be a "circuit preacher," but I wouldn't give it up for anything — except the Lord.

I love my work, it is my whole life. But it is taxing, it makes demands upon a person. Sometimes I get up in the morning and it is raining outside and my bed looks so inviting — but I've got a plane to catch. Or it's a beautiful sunshiny day outside and as I walk by the hotel swimming pool everybody else is lying around relaxing and getting a tan. And there I am off to who-knows-where to preach again.

My life is so regimented, I have to schedule a vacation. If I didn't put it on my calendar, I wouldn't get one. And even then sometimes I don't. When my family and I do manage to get away for a while, likely as not someone will hear I'm in town and the next thing I know I'm scheduled to preach a series of meetings. I'll look down from my hotel window and see my wife and kids down by the pool, suntanning. And there I am up on the eleventh floor preparing a sermon! I'm not complaining, but it does take commitment to do what I do.

So in a life like mine, sometimes a change of pace is a welcome blessing. I love to be around people, but there are times when I like to get away from it all for a while. This was one of those times. I got on that motorcycle and took off around that lake, and the peace of God came upon me like a blanket; it was wonderful.

Later I went back to the house and told Carolyn, "Get dressed; you've got to go for a ride with me!" So she got dressed and crawled up behind me on the motorcycle and away we went. We rode out by the lake and had a picnic there, just the two of us. What a blessing!

Two full months went by before I had a chance to ride it again — for about thirty minutes. And again the peace of God came all over me. It was so wonderful it began to bother me.

I said, "Now, Lord, You gave me this nice motorcycle and I appreciate it. But I don't really *need* it. I do enjoy it, but I don't get to ride it much. Most of the time it just sits in my garage. For someone else it might be a means of getting back and forth to work. What is to me just a toy might help somebody else make a living."

I had a sports car the Lord had given me, and I felt the same way about it. I enjoyed driving it, but every time I got in it I felt guilty. I felt bad even owning it. Especially since I didn't get to drive it except on rare occasions.

And that wasn't all that bothered me. I love animals, I love cattle and horses. Since we live out in the country, we have enough room to keep some horses and I love to ride them. But they weren't getting ridden much by me because I'm seldom home long enough to go for a ride. When you only have one day off in a blue moon, it's hard to do everything you want to do — drive your sports car, ride your motorcycle, go horseback riding, and still go to the office and get some work done!

So all these things I owned really began to bother me. I went before God. I said, "Lord, now I want to know about these things You've blessed me with. I am deeply grateful for them, but their only importance is the fact that they came from You. Other than that, they have no value to me whatsoever. I can give them away without batting an eye.

"What should I do about them? I don't want anything in my life to come between me and You. I don't want to own anything that is going to take priority over our relationship together."

Very gently the Lord spoke to me: "I haven't noticed that anything has."

"Well, Lord, I'm not taking any chances," I said. "I'm getting rid of these things right now."

"No, son," He said quietly, "I don't want you to do that yet."

"Why not?" I asked.

"Because I gave those things to you to enjoy. If you don't use them but one minute a year, the joy that you get from that one minute pleases Me."

I just melted. When I got home I was going to tell Carolyn what had happened. As I walked in, she met me at the door and said, "Jerry, God told me He doesn't want you to get rid of those things. He said that if you don't get to use them but one minute a year, that brings pleasure to Him." I almost passed out!

Less than a week later God gave me another sports car. "Lord, You are going to get me in trouble," I protested. "Why are You doing this?"

"Because I know your heart," He responded gently.

I want you to know, that statement meant more to me than the finest Mercedes ever built. More than a Rolls Royce or a half-million-dollar home. It meant more to me than any material thing in this world to hear God say to me personally, "I know your heart."

Give Your Heart to God

God is not against our having things. He just doesn't want things having us.

When God starts blessing you with things, if you are not careful it is very easy to start serving the things instead of the One Who gave them to you. That's why we have to be constantly on the alert against seeking God's provision rather than God Himself. I don't think it is enough to just check our heart once a year or whenever we get to feeling bad. No, I believe we should do it daily, because there is daily input from the adversary. Every day we live there is an opportunity to get off base, to get our priorities out of line. We ought to be in constant contact with our Source. We must continually commune with the Lord.

The writer of Acts tells us that the first disciples, **continuing daily with one accord in the temple, and breaking bread from house to house, did eat their meat with gladness and singleness of heart**

(Acts 2:46). God will give us each day our daily bread. He will do much more than that; He will bless us beyond our wildest dreams. But He wants our heart.

6

Unconditional Love

And the people answered and said,
God forbid that we should forsake the
Lord, to serve other gods;

For the Lord our God, he it is that
brought us up and our fathers out of the
land of Egypt, from the house of bondage, and which did those great signs in
our sight, and preserved us in all the way
wherein we went, and among all the
people through whom we passed.

Joshua 24:16,17

Sometimes our servitude is conditional. It is based on what God has done
or will do for us. Our love toward Him
is expressed in conditional terms: "I love
You *if* . . . ."

God doesn't love us *if*, He loves us
regardless. True love, real love, is always
unconditional. That's why God commands that our love for Him not be

conditioned upon His blessings, what He either has done or will do for us. God wants us to love Him as He loves us, regardless.

You see, the reason we are conditional about our love for God is because we are conditional about our love for each other: "I love you, *if* you agree with me, or behave like I want you to, or meet my standards or come up to my expectations."

Many times husbands and wives display that attitude toward each other, (whether they come right out and say it or not): "You'll have a hot meal (I'll love you), *if* you get home on time; otherwise, you'll just have to eat it cold!" "You can buy that new dress you want (I'll love you), *if* you don't cross me; otherwise, you can forget it!"

Likewise, parents and children demonstrate that same attitude toward each other: "You'll start having a few privileges around here (I'll love you), when you start showing a little respect for your elders!" "I'll straighten up (I'll love you), when you quit treating me like a kid!"

We human beings, Christians and non-Christians, try to dole out our love in proportion to the degree we think the other person "deserves" it. That's one reason we find it hard to believe that God doesn't "reward" us with His favor in the same way. We naturally assume that God is as conditional with His love as we are with ours. Which is one reason we sometimes try to "make deals" with the Lord.

I remember trying to make a deal with God once. It proved to be such a traumatic experience, I never did it again.

When I was a teenage boy I was involved in athletics and had a desire to be the greatest pole-vaulter in the world. I wanted to break the high school record, even the world record, for the pole vault. I had been practicing all summer and could hardly wait for track season to begin. Finally, it came around.

The day before it was to open I knelt down at my bed and prayed, "Lord, if You'll help me break the record, if You'll make me the greatest pole-vaulter in the world, I'll serve You."

The next day, the opening day of the new season, I was practicing my jumps when I fell and broke my leg. That settled my chances of being "world champion" in a hurry!

But the sad thing was that I thought it was God Who had done it to me because I had tried to make a deal with Him. So for a long time after that, I had a bad image of God. I would tell people, "Don't try to make any deals with God or He'll break your leg!"

Then one Sunday morning I didn't go to church because I had decided to stay home and work on my car. I had it jacked up on stands and was down underneath it pulling the transmission, when it suddenly fell off the stands. If I hadn't been so skinny, it would have crushed me.

Instead of thanking God for saving my life, I blamed Him for the accident. I figured He was mad at me for not going to church. He had only broken my leg the first time, I reasoned, now He was determined to "do me in." Needless to say, I had a very poor concept of God and His ways.

Many people today have the same misconception of God. They think He is "out to get them" for their sins. Or they think if they don't serve Him they will "suffer" for it. Their servitude is thus not motivated by love, but by fear.

Then there are those who serve God because of what they think He will do for them in return. If you are serving God for reward, you are in for a rude awakening. It's not going to be long before you have an opportunity to back off of that commitment, because the devil will come in and try to foul up your life, then lay it off on God. He will make it appear that it is God Who is causing you to suffer. The next thing you know you'll be taking backward steps.

We cannot serve God out of a sense of fear or out of selfish motives. We must serve God because we love Him. We must serve God, not from a sense of obligation or duty, but from a sense of love. We must do it because He loves us, and because we love Him.

When we love God so much that we give up everything else in order to serve Him, then we cannot give up and turn back because we don't have anything to turn back to.

True Service

The children of Israel were going to serve God because He had led them out of Egypt. Do you remember what happened in Egypt? God led them out of bondage, and before it got dark they were already griping and complaining and ready to go back and die.

They left Egypt, carrying with them all the gold and silver of their former masters. They went marching out in victory over Pharaoh. They were going to follow the Lord to the Promised Land! Then they got to the Red Sea, where they were caught between the sea on one side and Pharaoh's chariots on the other. As soon as they saw Pharaoh's army approaching from the rear, they immediately forgot how good God was to them and began complaining to Moses, "Why did you lead us out here to die at the hands of Pharaoh?" (Ex. 14:11.)

But God split the Red Sea and they crossed on dry land with Pharaoh's army right behind them. God closed the waters together and drowned the Egyptians so the children of Israel could cross over unharmed. Once on the other side, they held a celebration. They sang and danced for 21 verses! (Ex. 15:1-21.) When they had finished singing and dancing, they were hungry and there wasn't anything to eat. So again they started complaining to Moses, "Why did you lead us out here to die of hunger?" (Ex. 16:3).

So then God gave them manna from heaven. They ate it and became thirsty. Again they complained: "Why did you lead us out here to die of thirst?" (Ex. 17:3).

So God brought them water out of a rock in the middle of the desert. But still they were not satisfied. They kept on murmuring and complaining until finally God had to let that whole generation die off before He could find a group who would follow Him into the Promised Land.

The children of Israel served God only as long as He was doing something for them. Every time trouble came, they were quick to turn their heart away from God and murmur and complain. Some of their descendants are still with us today. Every church has its share. Ask any pastor.

It's not enough to serve God just because He has led us through trials and tribulations in the past. What are we going to do if serving God leads us to another Red Sea experience? Are we going to forget what God has done? Are we going to murmur and complain like the children of Israel?

No. We are to choose Whom we will serve, then stand by that decision through thick and thin, come what may.

God's love for us is unconditional. Our love for Him should be the same. God wants unconditional commitment, unconditional servitude.

7

Uncompromised Holiness

> And the children of Israel did evil in the sight of the Lord, and served Baalim:
>
> And they forsook the Lord God of their fathers . . . .
>
> Nevertheless the Lord raised up judges, which delivered them out of the hand of those that spoiled them.
>
> And yet they would not hearken unto their judges . . . .
>
> Judges 2:11,12a,16,17a

Just a few chapters back, before Joshua died, these people swore on an oath that they would serve the Lord and Him alone. Yet here we see that despite God's continual intervention on their behalf, they would not obey Him or the ones He set in authority over them. Obviously their pledge of loyalty and fidelity to God was in word only.

The modern-day Church has been in danger of this same failure. For the most part, today's Christians have not been sufficiently taught about holy living, consecration and servitude to God. I believe the Lord is bringing that teaching forth right now, just as He has recently done with faith.

For years most Christians did not know anything about faith. So God sent a revival of faith teaching. As a result, we have learned how to use our faith. I believe we now have a good grip on it. That is good.

Now we need to learn something about holy living, consecration and servitude. That is the reason for this book. But it is only the beginning of a wave of teaching that will come forth on these subjects, because God has ordained it.

We have learned what faith is and how to use it; now we will learn what to use it for. God wants us to have that great thing called faith, not so we can serve ourselves with it, but so we can better serve Him.

There is a revival going on right now in the Church, a revelation of new truth and a renewing of old truth. God has told me, "Son, there are some new truths that are becoming established in the Church. And there are some old truths the Church has neglected in the past but which are now being renewed. This is My doing. I am combining these two fundamentals together in order to build a Church that is uncompromising both in faith and in holiness."

Respectability or Godliness?

In recent years, old-fashioned godliness has fallen on bad times. It has taken a backseat to respectability. Nowadays we Christians want to be respectable. We don't want the world to laugh at us. They have ridiculed us many times in the past because of our own misunderstanding of spiritual things, because we have confused godliness with "piety."

Now, God doesn't want us to conform to the world so they will respect us. Our Lord Jesus has told us that if we follow Him and His way the world will hate us. (John 15:19.) But He did not mean to imply by that statement that we should go out of our way to cultivate that hate. And, sad to say, many times that is what we Christians have done. By our sanctimonious, holier-than-thou attitudes and our ignorance and fanaticism we have provoked the world's hate. That is not the way to win the world to our God.

Our Father made this world and everything in it. He ought to know better than anyone else how it works. We Christians should have been availing ourselves of that knowledge long ago. If we had, by now we would have the attention of the world.

If the Church of Jesus Christ had not gone to sleep for so many years, if we hadn't turned a deaf ear to God and His instructions, by now the world would be sitting up and taking notice of us. It would be coming to us for answers, instead of us having to go to it for ideas, because we would have been doing things right, whatever the field of endeavor — medicine, technology, economics, government, education, every aspect of public and private life. Even fashion.

We Christians ought to be trendsetters instead of trend-followers. We ought to be setting the pattern which the world follows, instead of the other way around. The Bible tells us to adorn the Gospel of Jesus Christ. (Titus 2:10.) To make it attractive, beautiful, appealing. To cause it to draw people. God doesn't want us to look or act like cavemen. He wants us to reflect well upon our Creator, our heavenly Father.

Believers ought to be fashionable. God doesn't want us looking like a bunch of refugees from the city dump while the rest of the world is keeping up with the times. The world ought to be looking to us Christians to set the standard. They should be watching us, how we dress and conduct ourselves. The world should be taking its cue from us, not vice versa.

God happens to be Number One. He sets the trends. As His children, we ought to be helping Him set them instead of following the trends of the world.

The Apostle Paul tells us in Romans 12:2:

> **Be not conformed to this world, but be ye transformed by the renewing of your mind, that ye may prove what is that good, and acceptable, and perfect, will of God.**

In the early days, the Church realized that Christians shouldn't conform to the world, so they tried their best not to look or talk or act like the world. In their zeal not to conform, they pushed non-conformity to the extreme. As a result of their one-sided view, they did not make the Gospel attractive. On the contrary, they gave the world a very distorted picture of what a Christian is supposed to look like and be. They presented an image of poverty, ignorance and fanaticism which was as unappealing as it was untrue.

Such well-intentioned but sadly misinformed Christians have tried so hard not to draw attention to themselves that they now stick out like a sore thumb. Such extremism does not adorn the Gospel at all, it makes it look foolish and repugnant.

As a reaction against this kind of negative presentation, many Christians have gone to the opposite extreme. They have gone to great lengths to adapt to the world's ways, to imitate it, to cultivate it. They are so afraid of appearing ignorant or fanatical or out of step with the times, they have adopted the world's values rather than remaining true to God. They care more about appearances than they do truth. In short, they are more concerned with respectability than they are with godliness.

But just because people go from one extreme to the other does not mean there is not a central truth. And that truth is that although we Christians are in the world, we are not of the world. While we are to go into all the world and present to it a positive, attractive Gospel, we are not to be influenced by the world. We are not to be conformed to the world, we are to conform it to the image of Jesus Christ.

Making Jesus Attractive

Many times when I am with people who aren't Christians, especially celebrities, I feel a bit "inhibited." Traveling as I do, I have the opportunity to meet a great number of people from all walks of life and from all levels, from the lowest to the highest.

Now, I have no trouble identifying with ordinary people whatever their background or level, but I must admit that sometimes associating with celebrities makes me feel a bit uncomfortable. I suppose it's only natural that in the presence of VIPs we want to make a good impression. We want them to think highly of us, to respect us. So we feel we have to be careful of what we say and how we conduct ourselves.

That is not only natural, it can be beneficial, as long as we make sure we are not more concerned with being respectable than we are with being godly. But there really should be no conflict there. As Christians we ought to always be "on our best behavior," so to speak. We ought always to strive to present to people, whatever their station in life, a pleasant and attractive image. As Christ's ambassadors, we represent the King of Kings and the Lord of Lords. We ought to make certain we do a good job of representing Christ so that others will be attracted to come to know Him too.

That does not mean that we should compromise our integrity or our Christian principles in an attempt to win the respect of men. There is a delicate balance to be maintained between fear of God and fear of man. Simply stated, we should always strive to maintain godliness, but in a way so as not to alienate ourselves from the very people who are in most need of that godliness.

For example, although I travel a great deal in my own private plane, I still fly commercially quite often. Many times I find myself seated next to a person who obviously does not know Jesus. He may be smoking or drinking or using profanity or even reading a lewd magazine. In such cases, if I allowed myself, I might feel uncomfortable or embarrassed even to sit there and read my Bible, much less to talk to him about my Lord. Yet at the same time, he is the very person who needs most to hear about Him.

So I don't let my natural, human insecurities rob me or him of God's best for either of us. But I am also careful not to approach him in a negative, judgmental way. If I do, I will lose him before I ever have a chance to reach him. This is where that delicate balance between godliness and compassion must be established and maintained. I must lead him to conviction of his need for God's love and forgiveness without seeming to condemn him for that need.

I usually approach it like this. Since I am careful to always appear in public well-dressed and well-groomed, people usually assume by my appearance that I

am some kind of professional person —
a lawyer, college professor or business
executive.

(One person once asked me if I was
in the oil business. "Why yes I am," I
replied honestly. After all, My Father
owns it all!)

I don't tell people that I am a preacher,
because that tends to make them uncomfortable and ill at ease; it stifles conversation. And conversation is exactly what
I am after. I certainly don't assume an air
of piety either: "Now, I'm a preacher, so
don't you smoke or drink or use foul
language in my presence!" If I did that,
I would destroy forever whatever chance
I might have had to win that person to
Christ.

No, I try to use tact, diplomacy,
wisdom. I remember that it is the Lord
Who draws them to Himself by His Holy
Spirit. I just sit there and mind my own
business. But since my business is
soulwinning, I silently pray for that
person, asking God to move upon him.

More times than not, sooner or later that person will strike up a conversation. I've been through this so many times, I know the pattern perfectly by now. It will usually go something like this:

"Where are you going?"

"To Houston (or wherever)."

"Business or pleasure?"

"Both."

"Going to be gone long?"

"Oh, three or four days. You?"

"Just overnight."

Then comes the clincher: "What do you do?"

I never say, "I'm a preacher." Instead I say, "I conduct success seminars."

"Oh, really? Success seminars, huh? That's very interesting. How does that work?"

"Well, we usually go into a city and rent an auditorium where we conduct a series of meetings on successful living."

"Yes, but what principles do you use in your teaching?"

Now I've got him! "I base all success on the authority of the Word of God."

That's when the person puts out his cigarette. It never fails. Then the next thing you know, this fellow who looks as though he is on top of the world has started opening his life to me. It is not at all uncommon for me to lead him to the Lord before we get to our destination.

That approach works tremendously well for me. I have led many, many people to the Lord that way. I never try to argue with them or force them or even to manipulate them. I just present to them a positive, attractive image of happiness and success to which they are drawn for solutions to their own problems.

As Christians we are called to be fishers of men, but any fisherman can tell you that you catch fish with a *lure*, not a club. If we really want to reach people for Christ, we must present to them a

Christ of love and forgiveness and compassion, One Who cares for them and their needs.

No one who calls himself a Christian, no one who purports to represent Jesus Christ, has a right to turn people away from God by his words or behavior. We must be careful to reflect well upon our Lord and Savior, to make Jesus attractive to others.

The world is hurting today. People are suffering. Everything they have ever trusted in is falling apart right in front of their faces. The government, the economy, the educational system, the judicial system, even many times the Church.

People are desperately seeking solutions for their problems, provision for their needs, direction for their lives, hope for their future, stability and power and peace. We Christians are supposed to have the key to all those good things which the world needs and seeks. That key is a personal relationship with God through His Son, the Lord Jesus Christ.

But unless we are careful to give evidence of all those good things in our own lives, there is little reason to expect the world to want what we have. Especially if we assume a pious, holier-than-thou attitude and sit in judgment upon them.

Christians are not sent to judge or criticize or condemn. But while we are not to condemn unrighteousness and ungodliness, we are also not to condone it. And we certainly aren't to join the world in it.

Jude tells us:

> **Be merciful to those who doubt; snatch others from the fire and save them; to others show mercy, mixed with fear — hating even the clothing stained by corrupted flesh.**

> **Jude 22,23 NIV**

We Christians are called to holy, righteous living. We are to live godly lives. We are not to condemn the world, but at the same time we are not to allow the world's attitude to creep into the Church.

Life Abundant

God has not given us rules, regulations and laws to bind us, to make us miserable, to rob us of life. Some people think that to serve God is not to have anymore fun in life. Dear me, I didn't know what fun was until I met Jesus. He is lots of fun. It just depends upon what one's definition of fun is.

That's the problem with many people today. Their idea of fun has been warped. As a teenager, my idea of fun was determined by the world. If I wasn't doing what everyone else was doing, then I thought I wasn't having a good time. But then I learned to let Jesus define fun for me, and I really began to come alive. Now I am having more fun than ever before in my entire life. And I don't miss for a second all those things I used to think were so enjoyable.

The Bible speaks of enjoying the pleasures of sin **for a season** (Heb. 11:25). That's the problem with sin. It may seem like fun for a while, but it only lasts a season. Sooner or later the new wears off and it takes something else to produce the same pleasure. More alcohol. Stronger drugs. More perverted sex. This is just the trick of the devil to draw people deeper and deeper into corruption and destruction. The trouble with sin is where it leads, what it produces: **For the wages of sin is death . . . .** (Rom. 6:23a).

But when a person serves God, he discovers what fun is really all about. I am enjoying more of the things of life, even the material things of life, now that I am serving God, than I ever did serving the devil.

Our holiness must be uncompromised. But holiness and happiness — righteous living and abundant living — these are not mutually exclusive terms. In fact, they go hand in hand. Jesus said: **The thief cometh not, but for to steal, and to kill, and to destroy: I am come that they might have life, and that they might have it more abundantly** (John 10:10).

While it is true that the wages of sin is death, the last part of that verse tells us, **. . . but the gift of God is eternal life through Jesus Christ our Lord** (Rom. 6:23b).

Life, eternal life, abundant life, life in all its fullness is ours through Jesus Christ. To live in holiness is not to forfeit life, it is to receive life, to discover life, to live life to the fullest.

8

You Cannot Serve
Two Masters

**And Joshua said unto the people, Ye
cannot serve the Lord: for he is an holy
God; he is a jealous God . . . .**

Joshua 24:19

God will not share His people with
other gods, whatever those gods may be.
God will not accept from His people a
divided heart. Either we serve Him, or we
don't. There is no middle ground. That's
why we are told to choose whom we will
serve, once and for all.

Jesus said that we cannot serve two
masters. Jesus considers serving the Most
High God the "high life." He says that if
we will let go of the "low life," He will give
us the high life we really want. He called
it the abundant life. (John 10:10.) Living

the full, abundant life of God is what
being a Christian is all about. I like to refer
to it as Adventures in Faith.

The Bible says that God is a holy God.
Since we are partakers of His divine
nature, God expects holiness out of His
people. He has every right to expect that
we walk worthy of Him Who has called
us into His kingdom and glory. (1 Thes.
2:12.)

Witnesses Against Yourselves

And the people said unto Joshua,
Nay; but we will serve the Lord.

And Joshua said unto the people, Ye
are witnesses against yourselves that ye
have chosen the Lord to serve him. And
they said, We are witnesses.

Now therefore put away, said he, the
strange gods which are among you, and
incline your heart to the Lord God of
Israel.

And the people said unto Joshua,
The Lord our God will we serve, and his
voice will we obey.

Joshua 24:21-24

Now I am sure these people meant well when they made this commitment to serve the Lord. But when the pressure came, they turned their back on God. When it came down to a choice between serving God and conforming to the world, they chose conformity.

Do you remember when Jesus called His disciples? He said, **Follow me, and I will make you fishers of men** (Matt. 4:19). He began to share with them how He would set up His kingdom, and it was exciting to them. They were ready to follow Him anywhere. They really thought He was going to establish an earthly kingdom right then with them as rulers over it. That idea appealed to them immensely. So they followed Him everywhere.

But did you also notice that when things began to get a little difficult, **many of his disciples went back, and walked no more with him** (John 6:66)? That is one of the things about human nature. It is easy for us to make a commitment when things are going well, when it looks as if it will benefit us. But when that commitment starts making demands upon us, it is very easy to back off, to turn back and walk no more with Him.

That is what the children of Israel did with God. Time and time again. They would make a solemn vow of faithfulness to the Lord. Then as soon as the pressures came, they would turn away and conform to the inhabitants of the land.

Did you know, for instance, that it was never God's will for Israel to have a king? He wanted to be their king. But the people would not hear of it. They wanted to have an earthly king over them. Why? Because that's what the other nations around them had. As is so often the case with us, they wanted to conform to other people more than they wanted to conform to the will and plan of God.

That is the way some people are today in the Church. They don't want God's rulership. They don't really want to do things His way. They want to be like other people. Oh, they might not ever come right out and turn their back on God. They just sort of want to hang on to God with one hand, and the ways of the world with the other. But that won't work. God says, "No, either you do it My way, or you don't do it My way." That's why He forces us to make a choice: either He is God, or we have a god of our own choosing.

Did you ever notice that every time God's people wanted to be like everyone else, it got them into trouble? More trouble than they could get out of by themselves? But then they would cry unto the Lord, and He would hear their cries and deliver them out of their destructions. Then after a while they would get right back into the same mess; they would cry unto the Lord, and He would hear and deliver them. This took place over and over again. The people just never seemed to learn.

With their example as a lesson to us, we should not make the same mistakes those people made. We should be wiser than that. Are we?

We would say, "Oh, but we don't turn away to other gods." No, not to idols and graven images. But we do most certainly have other gods.

When the pressures of life come, how many people do you know who run to the television? Have you yourself ever been tempted to give up the fight and just "stay home and watch TV like everybody else"? Have you never been tempted to just take your armor and shield and sword and throw them into a corner somewhere and seek relief in a bit of relaxation in front of the tube? Many Christians have, I can assure you. They get to the place where it seems that it is not worth the fight any longer, so they just give up and find their release in a little harmless "entertainment." They turn on the television and turn off the Lord. They choose whom they will serve.

Others do the same thing with hobbies. How many "sun worshippers" do you think are found at the lake or the beach or the golf course on any typical Sunday morning? And how many of those worshippers are supposed to be followers of the Most High God? They too have chosen whom they will serve.

Now don't misunderstand. There is nothing wrong with any of these things in themselves. But when we put anything, whatever it may be, in place of God, that thing becomes our god. And the Lord has made it clear that He is a jealous God — He will not share us with any other god.

But the choice is ours. After all, we are not robots. Serving God does not mean that we lose our will. It just means that our will should become conformed to His will.

I haven't lost my will. I still have freedom of choice. It's just that the things I choose now are in a different category from the ones I chose before I came to know Jesus Christ. Yet I am perfectly happy with my new choices, much happier than I was with my old ones.

As you feed your spirit on the Word of God, His will, His desires get down on the inside of your heart. As you keep feeding on that Word, you begin to find yourself choosing those things that please Him rather than those things that please someone else, or those things that satisfy your own selfish desires.

You may be surprised at the change which occurs in your own heart. You may find yourself wanting to do things you would never have thought possible before. What is happening is that your will is being conformed to His will.

Paul tells us, **For it is God which worketh in you both to will and to do of his good pleasure** (Phil. 2:13). Obedience to God becomes an act of our will, something which we desire to do from within, rather than a law or rule which is imposed upon us from the outside. When that happens, service to God is a pleasure, not a chore.

But in order for that to happen, we must be willing to be made willing. We must allow God's Holy Spirit within us to work His perfect work. We must continually yield ourselves to His will and desire. We have to be cautious not to let other things become gods over us.

Be Ye Stedfast, Unmoveable

This know also, that in the last days perilous times shall come.

For men shall be lovers of their own selves, covetous, boasters, proud, blasphemers, disobedient to parents, unthankful, unholy,

Without natural affection, trucebreakers, false accusers, incontinent, fierce, despisers of those that are good,

Traitors, heady, highminded, lovers of pleasures more than lovers of God.

2 Timothy 3:1-4

We are in the last days. The last days began almost 2,000 years ago when Peter stood and proclaimed: **But this is that which was spoken by the prophet Joel; And it shall come to pass in the last days . . . .** (Acts 2:16,17). Ours is a dispensation which began on the day of

145

Pentecost. So we have been in the last days for a long time.

"This know also, that in the last days perilous times shall come." The word *perilous* means "troublesome, hard, dangerous." I don't want you to think that just because such days are coming that we will be destroyed by them. God is warning us, He is letting us know that, yes, there will be troublesome times ahead. But that should not discourage us; rather it should motivate us all the more to prepare for those days, prepare to do something about them.

We have troublesome times right now. Everything seems to be crumbling all around us. We can no longer depend upon those institutions we once thought to be "rocks of Gibraltar." Everywhere we look we seem to be faced with weakening walls, crumbling foundations, lowering standards. All this produces problems: economic problems, social problems, personal problems. If we are not careful, we will be overcome by a feeling of futility and despair.

But there is something that can be done about all this. Much of the reason for all these problems is the fact that we in this country have lost contact with our spiritual roots. We in the Church have allowed ourselves to become more influenced by society, than we have been an influence for good upon society. That must change.

If our society ever regains its former greatness and soundness, it will be because its people have rediscovered their roots in Almighty God their Source. We in the Church have a great responsibility, a vital role to play in that rediscovery. We need to be in the forefront, setting the example of spiritual commitment that is needed to bring our society back to God.

We Christians need to quit fooling around and playing games. We need to get so established in God's Word that these things will not shake us.

In the Sermon on the Mount, Jesus described two men. One was a hearer of the Word only, the other was a doer of the Word. When the storms of life came, the "hearer only" had no foundation and so ended in destruction. But the man who was a doer of the Word underwent the very same storms, yet without harm. Because he had a firm foundation, he could not be shaken.

That is how God wants His people to be today: unshakeable, immoveable, stedfast, always abounding in the things of the Lord. (1 Cor. 15:58.)

We cannot serve two masters. If we are to save ourselves, and our society, we must build a firm foundation on the solid rock of God's unchanging Word.

9

Developing Holiness

But thou hast fully known my doctrine, manner of life, purpose, faith, longsuffering, charity, patience,

Persecutions, afflictions, which came unto me at Antioch, at Iconium, at Lystra; what persecutions I endured: but out of them all the Lord delivered me.

Yea, and all that will live godly in Christ Jesus shall suffer persecution.

But evil men and seducers shall wax worse and worse, deceiving and being deceived.

But continue thou in the things which thou hast learned and hast been assured of, knowing of whom thou has learned them;

And that from a child thou hast known the holy scriptures, which are able to make thee wise unto salvation through faith which is in Christ Jesus.

> **All scripture is given by inspiration of God, and is profitable for doctrine, for reproof, for correction, for instruction in righteousness:**
>
> **That the man of God may be perfect, throughly furnished unto all good works.**
>
> 2 Timothy 3:10-17

In this passage God is saying that even though everything seems to get worse, we are to continue in the things we have learned. As bad as our situation may appear, we are to remember that nothing can separate us from the love of Christ. Despite the difficult circumstances in which we may find ourselves, we are not to back away from our commitment. Solomon tells us:

> **When you make a vow to God, do not delay in fulfilling it. He has no pleasure in fools; fulfill your vow.**
>
> **It is better not to vow than to make a vow and not fulfill it.**
>
> Ecclesiastes 5:4,5 NIV

One translation of this passage says that it would be better to take a knife to your throat than to make a vow and break it. God is telling us in these verses that He wants commitment from His people. That is a word many Christians don't like, because they think they are supposed to be so "free." If we continue in that loose freedom, we may get to the place where God will set us free, *totally* free! I don't ever want to get in that position. I never want to get to the place where God says He is through with me, that He has done all He can do for me.

If we are to be useful to God, we must be committed to Him, obedient to Him. We must develop holiness. There are two basic steps to developing holiness.

Step One: Choosing God

See, I have set before thee this day life and good, and death and evil;

In that I command thee this day to love the Lord thy God, to walk in his ways, and to keep his commandments and his statutes and his judgments, that thou mayest live and multiply: and the Lord thy God shall bless thee in the land whither thou goest to possess it.

But if thine heart turn away, so that thou wilt not hear, but shalt be drawn away, and worship other gods, and serve them;

I denounce unto you this day, that ye shall surely perish, and that ye shall not prolong your days upon the land, whither thou passest over Jordan to go to possess it.

I call heaven and earth to record this day against you, that I have set before you life and death, blessing and cursing: therefore choose life, that both thou and thy seed may live:

That thou mayest love the Lord thy God, and that thou mayest obey his voice, and that thou mayest cleave unto him: for he is thy life, and the length of thy days: that thou mayest dwell in the land which the Lord sware unto thy fathers, to Abraham, to Isaac, and to Jacob, to give them.

Deuteronomy 30:15-20

God is insisting on a decision. There is life and there is death. Either we choose one or we choose the other. There is no in-between. God wants to know where we stand. He doesn't want to be in doubt where we are concerned. In this passage He tells us that we are to cleave unto Him. God doesn't want anything to be able to be wedged between us. He wants us to stick to Him like glue.

God wants 100 percent allegiance from us. If God has an unconditional commitment from us, He has promised to see to it that we will ride on the high places of the earth. (Is. 58:14.) There are benefits in serving God, but God wants us to serve Him whether there are any benefits or not.

We need more teaching on self-denial and consecration to God. God is saying He wants His people to be a holy people. The Bible says that without holiness we cannot see God.

We can't just pick and choose out of the Bible those passages we like. We must take God's full message. The same Bible that tells us that it is impossible to please God without faith also says that sin shall have no dominion over us. We need to know how to resist sin just as much as we need to know how to develop faith.

We cannot become the glorious Church God wants us to be without becoming more God-like. The less we know about holiness, the better it is for the devil. We need to talk about it, learn about it, get it down in our spirits, make a commitment to it.

It is to Satan's best interest to promote strife, bitterness, and contention so that the Church of Jesus Christ will not be able to operate in God's principles. We need a solid foundation. We need to have a thorough knowledge of holiness.

True holiness is to choose God.

Be ye not unequally yoked together with unbelievers: for what fellowship hath righteousness with unrighteousness? and what communion hath light with darkness?

And what concord hath Christ with Belial? or what part hath he that believeth with an infidel?

> And what agreement hath the temple of God with idols? for ye are the temple of the living God; as God hath said, I will dwell in them, and walk in them; and I will be their God, and they shall be my people.

> Wherefore come out from among them, and be ye separate, saith the Lord, and touch not the unclean thing; and I will receive you,

> And will be a Father unto you, and ye shall be my sons and daughters, saith the Lord Almighty.

> **2 Corinthians 6:14-18**

The first step in developing holiness is being willing to come out from among the crowd and choose God. The crowd is not going with God. It takes courage and commitment to stand forth and boldly declare: "I'm not going that way anymore." Repenting does not mean just feeling sorry. It means to turn and go in the opposite direction, to do exactly the opposite of what you were doing.

Proverbs 14:12 tells us: **There is a way which seemeth right unto a man, but the**

end thereof are the ways of death. And
our Lord Jesus Christ commanded us:
**Enter ye in at the strait gate: for wide is
the gate, and broad is the way, that
leadeth to destruction, and many there
be which go in thereat** (Matt. 7:13).

Any person who follows the world's
way is headed for destruction. Satan
paints a pretty picture along the way so
he can deceive those who follow him.
They may think they are following the
right path, but the Bible says that the end
of that path is destruction.

God does not paint us rosy pictures;
He does not play games with us. He
shows us the narrow way which leads to
life. He does not force us to choose it, but
His heart cries out that we will do so.

When we chose Jesus, we chose God.
That decision was Step One. Once we
have chosen God, then He gives us Step
Two.

Step Two: Perfecting Holiness

**Having therefore these promises,
dearly beloved, let us cleanse ourselves**

from all filthiness of the flesh and spirit, perfecting holiness in the fear of God.

2 Corinthians 7:1

Holiness is something that must be perfected. It is not something that happens to us overnight, which we then forget about for the rest of our life.

Sometimes we confuse holiness with righteousness. The Bible says that we are the righteousness of God in Christ Jesus. (2 Cor. 5:21.) We aren't going to become any more righteous than we already are. We can't perfect righteousness. We may become holier, but not any more righteous. We already possess righteousness, and that came about totally apart from us; it was a gift from God to us when we received His Son into our life.

But holiness is different. Holiness is a way of life to which we are commited the moment we choose God. In other words, righteousness is bestowed upon the children of God so they may live in holiness. But holiness is not automatic; it must be lived, worked out, moment by moment on a daily basis. It must be perfected. And a prerequisite for perfecting holiness is cleansing. There is no perfecting holiness without a daily cleansing.

Holiness is something we work on every day. There needs to be a daily cleansing of ourselves, because we come in contact with filth every day. We have to cast down imaginations every day, sometimes even hourly, because that's how often they come to us.

Holiness is the result of the continual cleansing of ourselves, flesh and spirit. This cleansing is not a one-time operation. Our environment is filthy. We are in the world, but not of it. We come into contact with filth every day, and it is highly logical that some of it will lodge in our mind. It must be removed before it has a chance to take root.

I once knew a great preacher who allowed himself to be enticed by the devil into watching a television show with just a little sex in it. Soon watching that show wasn't enough. He went out and bought some magazines. Then, when that didn't satisfy his growing lust, he bought a home video recorder and began to bring home pornographic movies. Then, when even that wasn't enough, he decided to try out what he had been watching.

Now that man has lost his church, his wife, and his family. And it all started with a little thought which the man did not cleanse himself of.

That is how all sin gets started, with a little thought that is not cleansed. In order to perfect holiness, we must be constantly on the alert to keep ourselves cleansed from the sin of the world.

Laying Aside Every Weight

Wherefore seeing we also are compassed about with so great a cloud of witnesses, let us lay aside every weight, and the sin which doth so easily beset us, and let us run with patience the race that is set before us,

Looking unto Jesus the author and finisher of our faith; who for the joy that

was set before him endured the cross,
despising the shame, and is set down at
the right hand of the throne of God.

For consider him that endured such
contradiction of sinners against himself,
lest ye be wearied and faint in your
minds.

Ye have not resisted unto blood, striving against sin.

Hebrews 12:1-4

Jesus is our way of perfecting holiness.
If we are looking unto Jesus while we run
the race set before us, we will not have
our eyes on filth. While we are running,
we are to lay aside every weight and every
sin. This is not a 100-yard dash we are
involved in; it is a lifetime race, a cross-
country race, an endurance race. In such
a race, we don't give it all we've got for
just a short distance.

We must pace ourselves for the long
haul. That way, as we approach the end
of our course, we will have something in
reserve for a strong finish.

That is the way God expects His Church to finish. Not beaten down, worn out and filthy dirty from the cinders where we have fallen down on the track. Our Father wants us to finish with a strong "kick" for glory.

I am looking unto Jesus every day, running the race that is set before me. As I run, weight and sin become attached to me. So I have to be sure to keep myself cleansed of those things because they interfere with my progress.

As we run the race of life, we must not keep running and running and never take time to cleanse ourselves of our accumulted weight and sin. If we do, it will keep piling up on us and make it harder and harder for us to complete our course. Unless we deal with the sin in our life, we will become so burdened down we can hardly run anymore.

That is what happens to many Christians. They give up, they drop out of the race, they turn their backs on God. Not because they no longer believe or no longer care, but because they have become so burdened down they simply cannot run any farther.

This passage tells us to lay aside every weight. How do we do that? How does one lay something aside?

A weight is an inanimate object. It has no life or movement of its own. Unless it is moved by an outside force, it will remain wherever it is placed.

If I removed my coat and laid it aside, unless moved by someone else, that coat would stay where it was placed until I took it back up and put it back on. It has no ability to get back on me. I must take it back upon myself.

So it is with sin. Sin cannot remain in a person's life unless he allows it to do so. It cannot get back on him unless he reaches for it, unless he receives it, entertains it. If he lays that sin aside and refuses to receive it back, it cannot abide in him or on him.

It doesn't matter how long a person has been committing a certain sin, or how long he has yielded himself to that sin. Once he makes up his mind to lay it aside, the battle is won. That sin cannot get back on him unless he reaches for it again. That's why the devil works so hard to tempt us and deceive us. Because he knows we have to choose sin, sin can't choose us. The only reason anyone ever sins is because he chooses to do so.

In order to sin, we Christians must take our eyes off Jesus. That's the devil's job, to get us to take our eyes off of our Lord so we will fall into sin.

There are sins in our lives that we haven't been willing to deal with effectively. We have conditioned ourselves to accept them.

I once had a sin in my life which my mind had been conditioned to accept. I felt bad about it, but my conviction was not strong enough to motivate me to put it aside. Every time the temptation would come I would get my eyes off of Jesus and yield to it. Until I became motivated enough within my spirit to make a quality decision to lay that sin aside once and for all, I was a victim of that sin.

But as Christians none of us is a helpless victim of sin. If we are victims, it's because we have allowed ourselves to be. God doesn't want us to be victims of sin. He doesn't want us to cover up our sin, or to give in to it. He wants us to deal with it, to get rid of it, to lay it aside. Daily cleansing and communion with God should be the aim of every believer. The result is a growth in holiness.

But what is true holiness?

Present Your Body A Sacrifice

I beseech you therefore, brethren, by the mercies of God, that ye present your bodies a living sacrifice, holy, acceptable unto God, which is your reasonable service.

Romans 12:1

God wants us to present our bodies as a living sacrifice. Our body is the housing of our soul and spirit. That is why God doesn't say, "Present your spirits as a living sacrifice." If we presented our spirit, it would not affect our body. But since the body is the temple of the soul and spirit, when we give God our body, we are giving Him our whole triune being.

Our bodies should be a living sacrifice, holy and acceptable, a reasonable service. Some Christians have read this verse, but have never done what it prescribes.

Be Transformed Within and Without

And be not conformed to this world: but be ye transformed by the renewing of your mind, that ye may prove what is that good, and acceptable, and perfect, will of God.

Romans 12:2

Did you notice that presenting the body as a holy sacrifice also involves the renewing of the mind? We have to have our mind renewed because what we have been taught basically by the world is not agreeable with God. In order to serve Him and run this race, we are going to have to do an about-face to the way the world thinks. We must not be conformed to the world's ways or their counsel, but be transformed by the renewing of our mind.

True holiness is the habit of being of one mind with God. It is not just how we dress. Our holiness is not determined by whether we wear gold or diamonds or make-up.

Many of the traditions of religion have kept women in bondage. Some have been taught that holiness means not cutting the hair. As though God judged the intents of the heart by hair length. Who would dare tell a woman today that if she cut her hair she would go to hell? Yet that has been the implication in many circles in the past.

Hair length has nothing whatsoever to do with inner holiness. God doesn't care how a woman wears her hair. He doesn't care whether she wears make-up or not. He doesn't care if she paints her face with Lucite house paint, as long as everything is right in her heart.

Let's not confuse religious observances or practices with true holiness. Let's not put people into bondage because of our personal conceptions (or misconceptions) of holiness. The foremost characteristic of holiness is a life devoted to God, one which is cleansed daily of all sin and weight, one which constantly looks unto Jesus, one which runs the race with eyes firmly fixed on Him. If we get in the habit of doing that every day, then eventually we will become of one mind with God.

That's what true holiness is — being of one mind with God. It is seeing things through God's eyes, taking God's Word for things.

David, a man after God's own heart, said of his Lord: **I esteem all thy precepts concerning all things to be right; and I hate every false way** (Ps. 119:128). That is the attitude of a holy man. Holiness is loving what God loves and hating what God hates. Holiness is measuring everything by God's standards.

Before we do anything, our attitude should be, "What would God think, what would God do?" Too many times we make our own judgments. We are not quick enough to ask God His opinion of the matter.

One of the functions of the Holy Spirit is to bring conviction. When we go against the will of God, a signal should be set off in our spirit. To ignore that signal is to choose sin. And to choose sin is to reject God.

Every day of our lives, we must make a choice between God and sin. Holiness is choosing God. It is agreeing with God, measuring everything by His standard. It is keeping God's Word and resisting every temptation to sin.

That is the reason holiness has to be perfected. That is the reason we are not yet perfect. Once we have conquered sin and set it aside, it is no longer a temptation to us.

There are some people who have won the victory over alcoholism. They used to be addicted to alcohol, but now it is no longer a temptation to them. They have perfected holiness in that area. But there may be another area in which they aren't yet perfected.

Alcohol may not be a problem to you, but you may be a worrier. If you worry all the time, you are not yet perfected in that area of your life. Worry is a sign of imperfect holiness, because God does not worry.

Once we ever get into the habit of thinking and acting and operating as God does, then we will have perfected holiness. It will not be easy to attain. It does not happen automatically or instantaneously. It will require effort and persistence on our part. But the end result is well worth it.

Mark the perfect man, and behold the upright: for the end of that man is

peace (Ps. 37:37). **Thou wilt keep him in perfect peace, whose mind is stayed on thee: because he trusteth in thee** (Is. 26:3).

If you would like to live in perfect peace, learn to perfect holiness.

Books by Jerry Savelle

You Can Have Abundant Life

Energizing Your Faith

*If Satan Can't Steal Your Joy,
He Can't Keep Your Goods*

Victory and Success Are Yours!

Sharing Jesus Effectively

Sowing in Famine

Fruits of Righteousness

God's Provision for Healing

New From Harrison House
Drawn By His Love
The Life of Holiness

Available from your local bookstore.

Harrison House
P. O. Box 35035 • Tulsa, OK 74153

Jerry Savelle is a noted author, evangelist, and Bible teacher who travels extensively throughout the United States. Jerry teaches the uncompromising Word of God with a power and authority that is exciting, but with a love that delivers the message directly to the heart. His down-to-earth approach and dynamic illustrations clearly present the absolute authority of God's Word.

At the age of twelve as Jerry was watching the healing ministry of Oral Roberts on television, God spoke to his heart and called him into the ministry. Several years later, on February 11, 1969, Jerry made Jesus Christ the Lord of his life. Since that time, he has been moving in the light of God's calling on his life. Prior to entering his own ministry, Jerry was an associate minister with Kenneth Copeland Evangelistic Association.

The scope of Jerry Savelle Ministries is far reaching as Jerry travels throughout the United States, Canada, Africa, Australia, and other parts of the world.

The anointing of God upon Jerry's life is powerful, and people are set free as the Word goes forth unhindered.

To contact Jerry Savelle,
write:

Jerry Savelle Ministries
P. O. Box 2228
Fort Worth, Texas 76113

*Please include your prayer requests
and comments when you write.*